Looking Back at the June 1967 War

Looking Back at the June 1967 War

Edited by
Haim Gordon

PRAEGER

Westport, Connecticut
London

Library of Congress Cataloging-in-Publication Data

Looking back at the June 1967 war / edited by Haim Gordon.
    p. cm.
    Essays presented at a conference held at Ben Gurion University of
the Negev, June 8–9, 1997.
    Includes bibliographical references and index.
    ISBN 0–275–96170–2 (alk. paper)
    1. Israel-Arab War, 1967—Occupied territories—Congresses.
2. Israel-Arab War, 1967—Influence—Congresses.   3. Arab-Israeli
conflict—Congresses.   4. Israel—Politics and
government—1967–1993—Congresses.   I. Gordon, Hayim.
DS127.6.O3G67   1999
956.04'6—dc21   98–37154

British Library Cataloguing in Publication Data is available.

Library of Congress Catalog Card Number: 98–37154
ISBN: 0–275–96170–2

First published in 1999

Praeger Publishers, 88 Post Road West, Westport, CT 06881
An imprint of Greenwood Publishing Group, Inc.
www.praeger.com

Printed in the United States of America

The paper used in this book complies with the
Permanent Paper Standard issued by the National
Information Standards Organization (Z39.48–1984).

10 9 8 7 6 5 4 3 2 1

For Claude Roche

A dear friend, who generously participates
in the struggle for peace and justice
in this troubled area of the world.

Contents

Preface

The essays gathered in this volume were presented at a conference held at Ben-Gurion University of the Negev on June 8–9, 1997. The conference convened Palestinians and Israelis who together looked back at three decades of their history. The keynote speaker was Noam Chomsky. Not all the papers presented at the conference are included in this volume, yet the general theme that prevailed at the conference is articulately presented in the chapters of this book. I want to thank Nahum Finger and Jimmy Weinblat for their support in organizing the conference. I also want to thank the organizations and the people who financially supported the conference: Ben-Gurion University of the Negev, The Israel Center for Peace in the Middle East, Hanan and Batia Guggenheim from St. Gallen, Switzerland, and the Foundation for Democratic Education in Israel.

Introduction

Haim Gordon

Wars are often viewed as turning points in history. The June 1967 War between Israel and its Arab neighbors, Jordan, Egypt, and Syria, was in many respects such a landmark. One major aspect of this turning point forcefully emerges in this book: following the war, Israel became an oppressive occupying power, ruling more than a million Palestinians in territories that it captured. Using military strength, and with the tacit agreement and support of the United States and other Western democracies, for thirty years Israel daily exploited and oppressed the Palestinians living in the areas it had occupied in 1967, in the Gaza Strip and the West Bank. Israel brutally suppressed their civil and human rights and trampled under foot their political rights. In a word, Israel denied the Palestinians their freedom. Unfortunately, during the three decades since 1967, many Jewish citizens of Israel accepted and supported these evil policies and ignored the injustices done in our name.

Plato's dialogues and the Bible agree on one pertinent point. A person, a society, or a polis who act unjustly are bringing ruin upon themselves. In Plato's dialogue *Gorgias* Socrates states emphatically that it is better to suffer wrong than to do wrong (*Gorgias*, 469). The Hebrew prophets continually admonished their listeners to refrain from doing evil, since such acts destroy their souls and their relationship to God. Despite this cultural and religious heritage, during the thirty years of Israeli occupation and brutal oppression of the Palestinians in the Occupied Territories, it was only infrequently

that the ruinous results of these actions were spelled out in any de-
tail in Israeli academic or religious circles. This book is therefore
very much of a first attempt to look back at these thirty years and
examine what happened to Israeli and Palestinian society and existence during this period. For many of the scholars contributing to
this volume, such looking back offered an opportunity to describe
and evaluate the injustices done to the Palestinians, to examine the
sources and the manifestations of these injustices, and to show
some of their sad results in Israeli and Palestinian society.

It would be a gross mistake, however, to view this modest book
as a mere scholarly description and evaluation of the many unfortunate developments in the Middle East, and especially between
Israel and the Palestinians, during the thirty years following the
June 1967 War. The careful reader will soon discern that this book
also contains an assault against the lack of a humane vision,
against the widespread indifference to injustices, and against the
crass oppression and exploitation that prevail in this area of the
world. Each chapter points out, explicitly and implicitly, that for
the peoples of this area life should have included much more freedom and happiness; their lives should have and could have been
much more promising. Such could have occurred, the authors suggest, if persons and leaders had been willing to see the truth star-
ing them in the face, had decided to think about these truths, and
had made the courageous decisions required by these truths. Put
otherwise, if justice and freedom had been respected by all those
involved in the political struggles of this region, much would have
been different. Consequently, the chapters blend to create a critique
of the prevailing *Realpolitik* in the Middle East and the world—a
political approach that is very much based on fear, greed, and lust
for power. Indeed, this political approach is ruinous for freedom,
for justice, and for a worthy and spiritual human existence. The authors, however, also point to a possibility for a better future; such
may evolve if the peoples of this region and those in power change
their insidious and pernicious approaches to politics, and, in a
word, seek justice.

Also unique to this modest book is its combining of papers dealing with scientific social research and essays based on diverse philosophical perspectives. Such an approach is quite rare, due to the
ongoing compartmentalization of academia. Indeed, it would be
rather difficult to find a book that blends global political analysis,
economic historical presentation, reports on psychological research,

Buberian critique of human relations, Wittgensteinian insights on the use of language, an attack on the poverty of postmodernism, and many other perspectives that clarify what happened during a specific period of history in a troubled area of the world. The diverse approaches do not compete or clash; nay, they complement each other. Thus, the chapters illuminate a spectrum that sheds a strong clear light on the many iniquitous decisions and unjust actions in this part of the world during the past three decades. This light reveals that these unjust decisions and actions rendered, among other ruinous outcomes, a multitude of unjust sufferings upon the Palestinian people; they also very much eroded the spirituality of existence of all peoples in the area, which in the past was the cradle of spirituality for the three monotheistic faiths.

Finally, this book has a humble yet worthy educational mission that transcends the presentation of the original thinking and research of its contributors. An entire generation has grown up in the Middle East and the world since the June 1967 War that has not known a reality whereby Israel is not an occupying and oppressing power. The book suggests that such a reality need not continue. It shows its readers that the future of the Middle East can change if we are willing to see the many wrongs we have done, wrongs that have characterized our existence during the past thirty years. After seeing these wrongs, we, and especially we Jews in relating to our Palestinian neighbors, must strive to exist differently. Indeed, this book suggests that only if we hearken to this simple message, which faintly echoes the resounding messages of the Hebrew prophets and of the other founders of the three monotheistic religions, can we, the peoples of the Middle East, hope for a more just and spiritually enhancing future.

Part I

Global Perspectives

I

The "Peace Process" in U.S. Global Strategy

Noam Chomsky

My primary concern here is the "peace process," its content, and its prospects. To summarize in advance, the Madrid-Oslo process should be understood, in my opinion, as an impressive vindication of the rule of force in international affairs, at both the policy and doctrinal level. The basis for this judgment, which bears directly on the prospects, should become clear, I think, when we attend to the actual terms of the agreements, and even more so, the general framework within which the process took shape. Needless to say, the influence of the United States has been overwhelming in this region for many years; not surprisingly, the Madrid-Oslo process is an expression of that fact. I will begin with a few remarks about U.S. global strategy, then narrowing the focus to the Middle East, and finally to the "peace process" itself, its origins and substantive content.[1]

I will keep to the period since World War II, when the United States became the dominant world power. It had been by far the largest economy in the world long before, but its global reach did not extend much beyond the Caribbean–Central America region and the Pacific (Hawaii and the Philippines).

Oil policy was an exception. In the late 1920s, the United States demanded and received a share in the control of Middle East oil, dividing these resources with Britain and France. Even earlier, the United States had moved to bar Britain, its major rival, from Venezuela, virtually taking over this richly endowed country, which was the world's leading oil exporter from the 1930s until 1970, and which, in the mid-1990s has again become the main source of U.S. oil imports, rivaling Saudi Arabia.[2] The United States itself was by far the main oil producer when Britain was expelled from Venezuela by the Woodrow Wilson administration, and remained so for almost half a century, but planning in this crucial domain has often been long-range.[3]

The basic principle of oil policy, enunciated by the Wilson administration and then more forcefully during World War II, was that the United States must maintain its "absolute position" in the Western Hemisphere, "coupled with insistence upon the Open Door principle of equal opportunity for United States companies in new areas." In brief, what we have, we keep, closing the door to others; what we do not yet have must be open to free competition. This is, incidentally, the way "free trade" and "open door" commonly function, in practice.

During World War II, Washington was able to displace Britain and France from the Western Hemisphere, establishing a regional system under its control in violation of the rules of world order it sought to impose elsewhere. The United States was at last able to achieve an early foreign policy goal excluding imperial rivals from the hemisphere under the Monroe Doctrine. The operative meaning of the doctrine was spelled out in internal deliberations of the Wilson administration. Secretary of State Lansing observed privately that "In its advocacy of the Monroe Doctrine the United States considers its own interests. The integrity of other American nations is an incident, not an end. While this may seem based on selfishness alone, the author of the Doctrine had no higher or more generous motive in its declaration." President Wilson found the argument "unanswerable," though he felt it would be "impolitic" to state it openly, particularly at this peak moment of American "idealism" in international affairs. With the doctrine finally imposed, Latin America was to assume its "role in the new world order": "to sell its raw materials" and "to absorb surplus US capital."[4]

The model is an important one to bear in mind when considering the Middle East, as recognized by Washington's British rivals/ allies, who understood its significance well enough. As World War II ended, Lord Killearn wrote that "I often wished that in years gone by we had followed America's wise example and established a sort of Monroe doctrine in this area," making it clear that we have "powder in the gun" and will "discharge it" if need be. A few months earlier, as Washington was again making clear to the British its intention to take over Saudi Arabia, the British Minister protested that "This is not Panama or San Salvador," so he erroneously thought, though (having little choice) "the British did acquiesce in American treatment of Saudi Arabia almost as if it were a Latin-American country," Wm. Roger Louis observes.[5]

After World War II, Washington sought to extend a version of the Monroe Doctrine to the Middle East oil-producing regions, in uneasy alliance with Britain. In accord with the Wilsonian interpretation, within the reach of the Monroe Doctrine and its extensions, the United States reserves the right to act as it chooses, without interference by the United Nations, the International Court of Justice, the Organization of American States (OAS), or anyone else. That position was reaffirmed recently when the United States rejected World Trade Organization (WTO) jurisdiction over its sanctions against Cuba in response to a complaint brought to the WTO by the European Union. The Clinton administration "argued that Europe is challenging 'three decades of American Cuba policy that goes back to the Kennedy administration,' and is aimed entirely at forcing a change of government in Havana," the Newspaper of Record reported.[6] The legitimacy of the goal is beyond controversy. Washington had taken the same stand in dismissing the order of the World Court to terminate its "unlawful use of force" (that is, international terrorism) against Nicaragua and to pay substantial reparations. On the same grounds, the United States has repeatedly barred UN resolutions calling on all states to observe international law, supported only by Israel (occasionally also Micronesia, Albania, or some other marginal actor), a regular pattern on a wide range of issues concerning world order and human rights. Israel's reliability is one sign of its dependence on the United States, which has no counterpart in world affairs.

Under Clinton, Washington has extended three aspects of the Monroe Doctrine to the Middle East as well. Secretary of State Madeleine Albright, then UN Ambassador, informed the Security Council that in this region, too, the United States will act "multilaterally when we can and unilaterally as we must," because "We recognize this area as vital to US national interests" and therefore recognize no limits or constraints, surely not international law or the United Nations.[7]

These are the prerogatives of overwhelming power. The "peace process" finds its place within this context.

Let us return to World War II, which left the United States in a position of global dominance with no historical parallel, possessing half the world's wealth and enjoying great advantages in every domain. Not surprisingly, "Following World War II the United States assumed, out of self-interest, responsibility for the welfare of the world capitalist system," in the apt words of diplomatic historian Gerald Haines, also senior historian of the CIA. As an executive of the Standard Oil Company of New Jersey phrased the matter in 1946, the United States "must set the pace and assume the responsibility of the majority stockholder in this corporation known as the world."[8]

The first postwar task was domestic. Articulating a broad consensus, the business press pointed out that advanced industry "cannot live without one kind or another of governmental support."[9] It was quickly realized that the Pentagon system would be the best device to socialize cost and risk while privatizing power and profit, in part because it is easy to disguise "subsidy" as "security," as the Truman administration observed. That has been the basis for most dynamic sectors of the economy ever since, and helps explain why the Pentagon budget remains at Cold War levels, currently increasing on the insistence of Congressional "conservatives," while social spending is cut.

The second postwar task was to reconstruct the industrial economies, restoring the traditional world order (including Nazi and fascist collaborators) while dispersing the antifascist resistance and its popular base. That should be Chapter 1 of a serious postwar history, beginning with Italy in 1943.[10]

In the case of Italy, as with of course Greece and Turkey, Middle East oil was an important concern. "US strategic interests" require control over "the line of communications to the Near East outlets of the Saudi-Arabian oil fields" through the Mediterranean, a 1945 interagency review observed, adding that these interests would be threatened if Italy were to fall into "the hands of any great power" (meaning, other than the United States). Washington took the matter quite seriously. The first memorandum of the newly formed National Security Council (NSC) secretly called for military support for underground operations in Italy along with national mobilization in the United States, "in the event the Communists obtain domination of the Italian government by legal means" in the 1948 elections. The influential planner George Kennan wanted to go further, outlawing the Communist Party, which was expected to win a fair election, even though he thought this would probably lead to civil war, U.S. military intervention, and "a military division of Italy."[11] Italy remained a prime target of CIA subversion at least until the 1970s, when the available internal record runs dry.

The commitment to subvert Italian democracy, a large factor in the enormous rise in corruption and crime, was not limited to government initiatives. The U.S. oil companies Exxon and Mobil, as well as Britain's BP and Shell, provided substantial funding to political parties, recognizing that their "best interests" would be served by "extending financial support to the major non-Communist Italian parties," as a Mobil executive put it. Foreign contributions to U.S. political parties are illegal, and when revealed, are considered a major scandal that undermines the democratic process. United States intervention in the electoral process abroad, which is massive in scale, is routinely praised as a generous contribution to democracy enhancement. The criteria are the same as those that define terrorism as "the plague of the modern age" when it is directed against the United States or its clients, but noble support for freedom fighters, or perhaps inadvertent errors or silly shenanigans that got out of hand, when agent and victim are reversed.[12]

Greece was officially recognized as part of the Middle East, not Europe, until the overthrow of the U.S.-backed fascist dictatorship in the 1970s. It was part of the peripheral region required to ensure control over Middle East oil, which the State Department described as "a stupendous source of strategic power, and one of the greatest material prizes in world history"; "probably the richest economic prize in the world in the field of foreign investment"—the most "strategically important area in the world" in Eisenhower's view, describing the Arabian peninsula. As Gendzier comments, "by 1947, the importance of the eastern Mediterranean and the Middle East to U.S. policy was beyond argument. Economic and strategic interests dominated calculations of U.S. policy, whether in Turkey, Iran, Saudi Arabia, Palestine, or Lebanon," while "to the consternation of British allies," the economic programs of the (highly selective) Open Door "locked the eastern Mediterranean and Middle East into U.S. foreign economic policy, if only because the region was both an indispensable source and a passageway" for oil. Concerns reached far beyond, not only to southern Europe but also to India, where "domination . . . by the USSR would be certain to cost us the entire Middle East," Eisenhower warned in 1954, referring primarily to trade and diplomatic relations, not conquest of course.[13]

The third postwar task was to restore the former colonial world to its traditional service role. Each region was assigned its "function" for the "welfare of the world capitalist system." High-level planning documents identify the major threat as "economic nationalism" ("radical nationalism," "ultranationalism"), which "embraces policies designed to bring about a broader distribution of wealth and to raise the standard of living of the masses," on the principle that "the first beneficiaries of the development of a country's resources should be the people of that country." These dangerous tendencies must be terminated: the prime beneficiaries are to be U.S. investors and their counterparts elsewhere, who must be assured a favorable climate for business operations and free access to the human and material resources of the service areas. In the Middle East, that translates to the concern that the people of the region might seek to be the beneficiaries of its enormous riches, which are to flow to the United States and its allies. The principles are spelled out frankly and explicitly in internal documents, which often have a vulgar Marxist tone, as is common in the business press as well.

The particular quotes just given,[14] which are typical, happen to concern Latin America, where there was not a remote hint of Soviet involvement at the time, just as there was virtually none in the Middle East. In later years, policies often became entangled in the Cold War conflict, but the basic thrust was essentially the same, and persists into the post–Cold War era with some tactical revisions, facts that are again important for understanding the "peace process."

How little things would change was revealed when the Berlin Wall fell in November 1989, ending any possible Cold War issue. The United States immediately invaded Panama, killing hundreds or perhaps thousands of civilians, installing a puppet regime of banks, businessmen, and narcotraffickers, vetoing two Security Council resolutions condemning the aggression and ignoring the condemnation of the OAS and the Group of 8 Latin American democracies, which had suspended Panama and now expelled it as a state under military occupation. Also ignored were continuing protests within Panama, including the client government's own Human Rights Commission, which years later continued to denounce the "state of occupation by a foreign army," condemning its human rights abuses.[15]

At the same post–Cold War UN session, Washington also vetoed a Security Council resolution condemning Israeli abuses in the Occupied Territories and (joined only by Israel) voted against two

General Assembly resolutions calling on all states to observe international law, one condemning U.S. military aid to the terrorist forces attacking Nicaragua,[16] the other its illegal embargo against Nicaragua. The United States and Israel were joined by Dominica in voting against a resolution opposing acquisition of territory by force, 151 to 3. The resolution once again called for a diplomatic settlement of the Arab-Israeli conflict with recognized borders and security guarantees, incorporating the wording of UN resolution 242, and the principle of self-determination for both Israel and the Palestinians, the latter unacceptable to the two rejectionist states.[17] I will return to the background of their unwavering rejectionism, now given formal status in the "peace process."

The Cold War was definitely over, but the U.S.–Israeli stand on international law, force versus diplomacy, human rights, and the UN remained unchanged.[18] Contempt for international law is so extreme that in the debate over the Panama invasion, the U.S. Ambassador informed the Security Council that the UN Charter permits the United States to use force "to defend our interests," eliciting no public comment.

The invasion of Panama was a mere footnote to history, apart from two innovations. First, it was not in "self-defense against the Russians," no longer available as a threat; rather, the motive was to capture the criminal Noriega—indeed a criminal, whose major crimes had been committed while he was on the CIA payroll, but who became an authentic criminal when he began to act too independently and was not cooperating properly with the U.S. war against Nicaragua. Second, as pointed out by former Undersecretary of State Elliot Abrams, with the Soviet deterrent gone, the United States was now able to "use force" more readily to attain its ends, opportunities that had been discussed earlier by U.S. policy analysts and that were causing no slight alarm in the Third World.[19]

The immediate reaction to the final end of the Cold War is instructive. Policies continued much as before, but with new pretexts and fewer constraints, effects soon to be seen in the Middle East as well. There were other continuities. President Bush took the occasion of the Panama invasion to announce still more assistance to his friend and ally Saddam Hussein. Shortly after, the White House submitted to Congress its annual budgetary request for the Pentagon. It was virtually unchanged, apart from justifications. In the "new era," the statement explained, "the more likely demands for the use of our military forces may not involve the Soviet Union and may be in the

Third World"—just as before, though now without invoking a Soviet threat. Furthermore, it will remain necessary to strengthen "the defense industrial base" (meaning most of the high-tech industry) and to create incentives "to invest in new facilities and equipment as well as in research and development," maintaining the public subsidy, but no longer because of the Soviet threat; rather, to counter "The growing technological sophistication" of the Third World—which the United States was seeking to enhance through sales of sophisticated armaments, with increasing fervor after the Gulf War, which was used frankly as a sales-promotion device. Military intervention forces must also be maintained, still primarily targeting the Middle East, because of "the free world's reliance on energy supplies from this pivotal region," where the "threats to our interests" that have required direct military engagement "could not be laid at the Kremlin's door," contrary to earlier doctrine, no longer functional. "In the future, we expect that non-Soviet threats to these interests will command even greater attention."[20]

In reality, the "threats to our interests" had always been indigenous nationalism, a fact recognized internally, and sometimes even publicly. We return to the matter. The "threats to our interests" could also not be laid at Iraq's door. At the time (March 1990), Saddam Hussein was a favored friend and trading partner, and remained so until August, when he committed the first crime that mattered: disobeying orders. He then lost the status of "moderate," which had been unaffected by such acts as gassing Kurds and torturing dissidents, a replay of the story of Noriega and many others.

In any event, with the fall of the Berlin Wall, it was at least conceded that the core "threat to our interests" has been independent nationalism, often with Cold War entanglements. One useful effect of the end of the Cold War is that the clouds have lifted somewhat and reality is coming into clearer view.[21]

Let us look more closely at how the Middle East falls into the general picture. The crucial issue has remained "history's greatest material prize." A high priority has been to assure that control over the world's cheapest and most abundant energy reserves are in U.S. hands. Immediately after World War II, France was unceremoniously expelled, on the interesting legal argument that it was an enemy country, having been occupied by Germany. Britain was permitted a subsidiary role. As one elder statesman of the Kennedy administration put it, Britain may "act as our lieutenant (the fashionable word is partner)."[22] Britain has preferred to hear the fashionable word, though its diplomats understood as the war ended that Britain would be no more than a "junior partner in an orbit of power predominantly under American aegis." The United States was already exercising "power politics naked and unashamed," going well beyond the traditional "spheres of influence" approach, British Foreign Secretary Ernest Bevin complained in internal discussion.[23] Foreign Office records reveal few illusions about "the economic imperialism of American business interests, which is quite active under the cloak of a benevolent and avuncular internationalism" and is "attempting to elbow us out." Americans believe "that the United States stands for something in the world," the minister of state at the British Foreign Office commented to his cabinet colleagues: "something of which the world has need, something which the world is going to like, something, in the final analysis, which the world is going to take, whether it likes it or not." Not an inaccurate perception, though not approved for public consumption.[24]

To organize and control the Middle East region, Washington took over the basic structure of the system that Britain had designed. Local management was assigned to an "Arab Facade," with "absorption" of the colonies "veiled by constitutional fictions as a protectorate, a sphere of influence, a buffer State, and so on," a device more cost-effective than direct rule (Lord Curzon and the Eastern Committee, 1917–1918). The Facade should receive only the "outward semblance of sovereignty," the High Commissioner for Palestine and Transjordan explained, describing the steps to evade UN demands for decolonization in 1946. But we must never run the risk of "losing control," as John Foster Dulles warned as the United States took over the British system.[25]

The conception is conventional. Similar ideas have guided U.S. policy in the Western Hemisphere, the USSR in Eastern Europe, South Africa in the Bantustan era, and the United States and Israel in today's "peace process," among many cases. Even outright colonies like India under the Raj were ruled in much the same way, by a local facade. The Facade must be dependable, therefore weak. In the Middle East, family dictatorships are preferred. They are tolerable, even honored, no matter how brutal their behavior, as long as they direct the flow of profits to the United States, its British lieutenant, their energy companies, and other approved projects. If they perform that "function," they are amply rewarded by the U.S. taxpayer, who knows nothing about it. To illustrate, "the amount of U.S. dollars flowing from the American treasury to Arab oil producers dwarfed the amount of U.S. foreign aid to Israel from 1950 until 1973," Yale University economic historian Diane Kunz observes, though the funds, based on tax manipulation, could be interpreted as a gift from the taxpayer to the oil companies. In comparison, even before 1967, Israel received the highest per capita U.S. aid of any country, a substantial part of the unprecedented capital transfer to Israel from abroad that constituted almost all of its investment, Harvard Middle East specialist Nadav Safran alleges. Kunz estimates "American private transfers to Israel" (much of it tax-deductible, hence U.S. government aid) at 35 percent of Israel's annual budget in the 1950s. Later the amounts were far greater.[26]

After 1973, the temporary rise in oil prices required measures to recycle petrodollars to the U.S. Treasury through arms sales, construction projects, and other devices, one reason why the United States did not particularly oppose the price increase, another being the extraordinary profits of U.S. oil companies as the oil price rose (along with other commodity prices, including major U.S. exports). These factors provided the United States with a positive trade balance with Middle East OPEC members in 1974–1975, also yielding huge profits for U.S. corporations and a flow of billions of Saudi dollars to U.S. Treasury securities.[27]

But since the Facade must be weak and compliant, a problem arises: the danger of internal unrest by populations that fall prey to the idea that they should benefit from the region's resources. The Facade must be protected from such "radical nationalism." That requires regional enforcers, local "cops on the beat" as they were called by the Nixon administration. These are preferably non-Arab: Iran (under the Shah), Turkey, Israel, Pakistan. It is understood that police headquarters remain in Washington, though the lieutenant can share the responsibility. As British military historian John Keegan explained when Britain joined the United States in the Gulf War, the British have a "sturdy national character" and a proper tradition: they "are used to over 200 years of expeditionary forces going overseas, fighting the Africans, the Chinese, the Indians, the Arabs. It's just something the British take for granted," and the new task "rings very, very familiar imperial bells with the British," who have always understood the importance of "reserving the right to bomb niggers," as the eminent British statesman Lloyd George expressed the common theme.[28]

Rights are assigned by virtue of the role that actors play within the system. The United States has rights by definition; Britain too, as long as it "acts as our lieutenant" (not in 1956, when it invaded Egypt without authorization, and was quickly expelled). The regional gendarmes and the Arab Facade have rights as long as they fulfill their functions. Those who contribute nothing to the system of power have no rights: Kurds, slumdwellers in Cairo, and others, among them Palestinians—who, in fact, have "negative rights," because their dispossession and suffering arouse unrest. These simple realities explain a good deal about U.S. policies in the region, including the "peace process."

Some useful instruction on these matters was provided by the influential neoconservative intellectual Irving Kristol. He pointed out that "insignificant nations, like insignificant people, can quickly experience delusions of significance," which must be driven from their primitive minds by force: "In truth, the days of 'gunboat diplomacy' are never over. . . . Gunboats are as necessary for international order as police cars are for domestic order." Kristol's ire had been aroused by Middle East upstarts who had dared to raise the price of oil beyond what the master ordered. More sweeping proposals for dealing with this insubordination were offered at the same time by Walter Laqueur, another highly regarded public intellectual and scholar. He urged that Middle East oil "could be internationalized, not on behalf of a few oil companies, but for the benefit of the rest of mankind." If the insignificant people do not perceive the justice and benevolence of this procedure, we can send the gunboats.

Laqueur did not draw the further conclusion that the industrial and agricultural resources of the West might also be internationalized, "not on behalf of a few corporations, but for the benefit of the rest of mankind," even though "by the end of 1973, U.S. wheat export cost three times as much per ton as they had little more than a year before," to cite just one illustration of the sharp rise in commodity prices that preceded or accompanied the rise of oil prices. Those who perceive an inconsistency need only be reminded of the crucial distinction between significant and insignificant people.

Palestinians are not only "insignificant people," but are much lower in the ranking, because they interfere with the plans of the world's most "significant people": privileged Americans and Israeli Jews (as long as they keep their place). Worse yet, instead of sinking into the oblivion that becomes them, "Palestinian Arabs [are] people who breed and bleed and advertise their misery," Ruth Wisse explained in the prestigious neoconservative journal of the American

Jewish Committee. That is "the obvious key to the success of the Arab strategy" of driving the Jews into the sea in a revival of the Nazi *Lebensraum* concept, she continued. Then a professor at McGill University, she moved to Harvard to take a chair endowed by Martin Peretz, who advised Israel on the eve of its 1982 invasion of Lebanon that it should administer to the PLO a "lasting military defeat" that "will clarify to the Palestinians in the West bank that their struggle for an independent st⸱⸱⸱ ⸱s suffered a setback of many years." Then "the Palestinia⸱⸱⸱ ⸱rned into just another crushed nation, like the K⸱⸱⸱ ns," and the Palestinian problem—which "i⸱⸱⸱ "—will be resolved.[29]

One cannot fully ⸱⸱⸱ rocess" without an appreciation of the cult⸱⸱⸱ arises, illustrated not only by such thoughts⸱⸱⸱ ntellectuals, but more significantly by the fact⸱⸱⸱ pa⸱⸱⸱ t notice, apparently being considered quite n⸱⸱⸱ tho⸱⸱⸱ ⸱⸱ge of a few names would elicit a rather different reaction.[30]

The general strategic conception explains the persistence of the huge military intervention apparatus aimed at the Middle East, with bases stretching from the Pacific, though the Indian Ocean, to the Azores. The unraveling of colonial relations has led to modifications in the system, but they are not very profound. A 1992 Congressional study found that Washington had made, or was in the process of making, "access agreements" with about forty nations (Israel prominent among them) as a more cost-effective device than foreign bases. Middle East oil remains a prime concern. Visiting the Philippines to establish such arrangements after the closing of U.S. military bases, Admiral Larson declared that "The Philippines may be used as a staging area for U.S. military operations should the U.S. initiate involvement in those areas" (Korea and the Mideast, where there are "brewing conflicts"). The Philippine defense minister expressed some concern that the Philippines might be "dragged into a war in the Mideast" as a result.[31]

Similarly, the end of the Cold War has led mostly to tactical modifications. At a peak moment of Cold War tensions in 1980, Robert Komer, the architect of President Carter's Rapid Deployment Force (later Central Command), aimed primarily at the Middle East, testified before Congress that its most likely use was not to resist a (highly implausible) Soviet attack, but to deal with indigenous and regional unrest ("radical nationalism"). The same analysis had been stressed internally. At another critical moment, in 1958, Secretary of

State John Foster Dulles informed the National Security Council that the United States faced three major foreign policy crises: Indonesia, North Africa, and the Middle East (all Islamic). He added that there was no Soviet role in any of these crises, and President Eisenhower took "vigorous exception" to the suggestion that others might be serving as Soviet proxies.

In Indonesia, the basic threat was democracy, as in Italy in 1948 and afterward: the fear that "Communists could not be beaten by ordinary democratic means in elections" and must be "eliminated," a program undertaken successfully a few years later, with the slaughter of some half-million people, mostly landless peasants, eliciting unconstrained euphoria in the West—a revealing glimpse of Western civilization, best forgotten, as it has been. In North Africa, the problem was the anticolonial struggle, which was interfering with the U.S. intent that "North African states under France's benevolent tutelage develop into friendly partners which will be bulwarks of a strong France" (the same "function" that the former colonies were to fulfill for "the welfare of the world capitalist system" generally). In the Middle East as well, the primary threat was "radical nationalism." As noted, the basic points are now publicly acknowledged.[32]

The system has worked well for half a century, a long period in human affairs. One index is the price of oil in the United States. It has changed very little in fifty years, reaching its lowest level in real terms in 1995,[33] though two qualifications are necessary. First, the United States does not want the price to fall too low, because that would cut into profits of the energy corporations, mostly U.S.-based, and would undermine important markets for arms, construction, etc. Second, the actual price is considerably higher than the official numbers indicate, because they fail to take into account many factors, among them, the cost of the military forces deployed to keep the prices within an acceptable range. The direct costs amount to a 30 percent public subsidy to oil prices, according to one technical study I know of, by a Department of Energy consultant, who takes the results to show that "the current view that fossil fuels are inexpensive is a complete fiction."[34] Estimates of alleged efficiencies of trade, and conclusions about economic health and growth, are of limited validity if we ignore many such hidden costs.

Though the system has generally been a great success, providing important underpinnings for the "golden age" of state capitalism in the postwar period, problems have arisen. The first was a nationalist uprising in Iran, quickly suppressed with a U.S.-backed military coup that restored the Shah. Full details of the operation will probably never be learned. The regular thirty-year archival declassification procedure (covering these events) was disrupted by Reaganite statist reactionaries, leading to the resignation of State Department historians in protest. More recently, it has been revealed that CIA records of the coup were "inadvertently" destroyed.[35]

A second problem arose when Britain, France, and Israel invaded Egypt in 1956. This was unacceptable to the United States, primarily because of timing according to President Eisenhower, who quickly forced the three disobedient countries to withdraw.

There were also continuing problems with Syria and Egypt, also leading to U.S. attempts to overthrow the regimes.[36] Secretary of State Dulles described Egyptian president Gamal Abdel Nasser as "an extremely dangerous fanatic." He was a fanatic because of his neutralism and independence, and dangerous because the people of the region are "on Nasser's side," President Eisenhower recognized ruefully. Our "problem is that we have a campaign of hatred against us, not by the governments but by the people," he added. By January 1958, concerns were becoming quite serious. The National Security Council concluded that "In the eyes of the majority of Arabs the United States appears to be opposed to the realization of the goals of Arab nationalism. They believe that the United States is seeking to protect its interest in Near East oil by supporting the *status quo* and opposing political or economic progress." Washington's basic problem was that the perception was correct. As the NSC formulated the matter, "our economic and cultural interests in the area have led not unnaturally to close U.S. relations with elements in the Arab world whose primary interest lies in the maintenance of relations with the West and the status quo in their countries." For reasons that are deeply rooted in policy formation and its institutional sources, the United States found itself on a collision course with independent nationalism, as elsewhere in the Third World.

These problems came to a head a few months later, in July 1958, when a military coup overthrew the British client regime in Iraq. United States–United Kingdom reactions give a clear picture of interests and intentions, and provide highly relevant background for what happened in 1990 when Iraq invaded Kuwait, with a significant impact on the "peace process," to which I will return. The United States immediately landed marines in Lebanon, with a presidential order to prepare for use of "*whatever* means might become necessary to prevent any unfriendly forces from moving into Kuwait" (Eisenhower's emphasis). Middle East scholar William Quandt, who also has a background in the national security apparatus, interprets this as a reference to the use of nuclear weapons. British Foreign Secretary Selwyn Lloyd flew to Washington for consultations. These led to a recommendation that Britain grant nominal independence to Kuwait while maintaining its virtual colonial status. The only alternative considered was immediate British occupation of Kuwait, an option rejected because it might arouse further nationalist reactions in Kuwait and elsewhere. But Britain must be prepared "ruthlessly to intervene" if anything goes wrong, "whoever it is has caused the trouble"—Kuwaiti nationalism, for example. Washington was to assume the same posture toward Saudi Arabia and the Gulf principalities, agreeing that "at all costs these oilfields [in Kuwait, Saudi Arabia, Bahrain and Qatar] must be kept in Western hands," Lloyd cabled to London.

Kuwait was assigned to Britain. As senior partner, the United States took charge of most of the rest. Washington recognized that the British economy relied heavily on the wealth of the region, and determined that the United States must be ready "to support, or if necessary assist, the British in using force to retain control of Kuwait and the Persian Gulf." The major difference in 1990 was that power had shifted even more to U.S. hands. The terminology should be noted: the United States and United Kingdom are to *retain control* of the oil producing regions, not to *defend* them. In public, there was a ritual appeal to the Soviet threat, but the internal record is again different. The perceived threat was the usual one throughout the service areas: "radical nationalism."

In January 1958, the NSC had concluded that a "logical corollary" of opposition to growing Arab nationalism "would be to support Israel as the only strong pro-Western power left in the Middle East," an exaggeration, which identified indigenous nationalism as the primary threat, as elsewhere in the Third World—with overwhelming clarity in Latin America and Southeast Asia.[37] The NSC analysis also affirmed the conclusions of the Joint Chiefs of Staff in 1948 when they were much impressed by Israel's military prowess and suggested that Israel might be a suitable base for U.S. power in the region, second only to Turkey, they felt.

Failure to look closely at the internal record, the timing of events, and the close similarity of policies throughout the world can easily lead to a misreading of their basic thrust, hence a dubious interpretation of current developments and prospects. One standard formulation is that "the Israeli-Arab conflict was fueled by the Cold War, in which the United States regarded Israel as a reliable ally against the Soviet-backed regime of some Arab states." I am quoting from an Israeli "post-Zionist" analysis, highly critical of standard interpretations, but in this case, not critical enough. The statement is not literally false, but is highly misleading.[38] Support for local "cops on the beat"—Israel, South Africa, and others—has regularly been seen as a "logical corollary" of opposition to indigenous nationalism in the service areas. The targets of subversion and attack often did turn to the USSR for support, sometimes for independent reasons as well, just as Islamic fundamentalist extremists in Afghanistan turned to the United States for support against Russian aggression. But the USSR did not attack Afghanistan in fear of United States support for Hekmatyar. We should be careful not to confuse cause with consequences, or to misconstrue the way the Cold War connections developed.

Much more accurate, in my opinion, is the interpretation of former chief of Israeli military intelligence Gen. Shlomo Gazit, who wrote after the collapse of the USSR that

Israel's main task has not changed at all, and it remains of crucial importance. Its location at the center of the Arab Muslim Middle East predestines Israel to be a devoted guardian of stability in all the countries surrounding it. Its [role] is to protect the existing regimes: to prevent or halt the processes of radicalization and to block the expansion of fundamentalist religious zealotry[39]

—no problem as long as it is properly disciplined (as in Saudi Arabia, Afghanistan, or for that matter in the United States itself, which ranks high in the scale of "fundamentalist religious zealotry"), but an unacceptable form of "radical nationalism" if it escapes these bonds, whether or not it turns elsewhere for support. In these terms, well supported by the documentary and historical record, we can understand the highly systematic character of policy, and its essential continuity with the USSR gone from the scene.

Returning to forty years ago, fear of the Nasserite disease did not abate. By the early 1960s there was concern that it might infect even Saudi Arabia, the ultimate domino in the region. Israel's military victory in 1967 put an end to these concerns, earning it the status of "strategic asset" that it has since maintained, and also arousing enthusiastic support for Israel among American intellectuals, much impressed by the effective use of force against people with "delusions of significance"—no small issue in those years of Washington's difficulties in Vietnam, and an important topic that I will have to put aside here.[40]

The aftermath is familiar. The "logical corollary" was translated into a major policy instrument. U.S. military and diplomatic support for Israel increased sharply again in 1970, when Israeli muscle-flexing deterred possible Syrian intervention in Jordan in support of Palestinians under brutal assault there, a possibility that the United States regarded as a threat to the Arab Facade. By the early 1970s, a de facto alliance was in place between Israel and Iran, the two major local gendarmes within the newly articulated Nixon Doctrine. The Senate's leading specialist on the Middle East and oil politics, Henry Jackson, described these partners as two "reliable friends of the United States," who, jointly with Saudi Arabia, "have served to inhibit and contain those irresponsible and radical elements in certain Arab States . . . who, were they free to do so, would pose a grave threat indeed to our principal sources of petroleum in the Persian Gulf"—sources that the United States then hardly used, but that were needed as a reserve and as a lever for world control, and for the vast wealth they yield. The formal conflict between Saudi Arabia and both Iran and Israel was only a technicality, as was the theoretical opposition of the Shah's regime to Israel's policies.

With the fall of the Shah in 1979, Israel's importance as a regional gendarme increased. After the failure of President Carter's emissary General Robert Huyser to inspire a military coup in Iran, the United States, Israel, and Saudi Arabia tried to restore the tripartite alliance, with Saudi Arabia funding the sale of U.S. arms via Israel to elements of the Iranian military, who, it was hoped, would overthrow the regime. The goals and intended measures were described with brutal frankness at the time by Uri Lubrani (effectively, Israel's ambassador to Iran under the Shah); also by Moshe Arens (then ambassador to the United States) and others.[41]

By that time, Israel's client relationship was firmed up on other grounds. Israel was performing important secondary services in Africa and Asia, but particularly in Latin America, where Washington was inhibited from providing direct support for the more brutal tyrants and killers by popular opposition and Congressional human rights legislation that reflected the popular mood. Carter, and increasingly, the Reaganites, were able to turn to Israel to take over such tasks by the 1980s, as part of an international terror network including also Taiwan, Britain, Argentine neo-Nazis, and others, often with Saudi funding. Israeli cooperation in weapons development and testing under live battlefield conditions was also a matter of increasing interest in Washington, along with basing facilities for the U.S. fleet and for prepositioning of weapons, contingency-planning joint exercises, and the like, again within the general strategic conception, and independently of the Cold War—hence persisting with no notable change. These matters are reported in Pentagon testimony to Congress and the writings of U.S.–Israeli strategic analysts. One interesting case is the analysis by Netanyahu's close associate Dore Gold, spelling out Israel's role as an intervention force in "non-Soviet scenarios"—that is, against "radical nationalism"—thus "expand[ing] the range of American options."[42]

Let us turn to the diplomatic record, which is eminently understandable in the developing context just outlined.[43] After the June 1967 War, the great powers established UN resolution 242 as the basic framework for a diplomatic settlement, calling for Israeli withdrawal from the conquered territories in return for a peace treaty between Israel and the Arab states. Though archival records are not yet fully available, enough has appeared—including a leaked State Department history—to establish that the United States understood UN 242 to require *full* Israeli withdrawal to the prewar borders, with at most minor and mutual adjustments, the position announced officially in the 1969 Rogers plan. Under Washington's interpretation, UN 242 called for full withdrawal in return for full peace. The Arab states refused full peace and Israel refused full withdrawal, settling in 1968 on the Allon Plan, which has undergone various modifications over the years. The Oslo agreements laid the groundwork for implementation of a contemporary version, with slightly different variants as political power shifts between Labor and Likud coalitions.

Note that UN 242 is outright rejectionist, with no recognition of any Palestinian right of self-determination. That fact is of crucial importance for understanding the U.S.-run "peace process." The impasse over UN 242 was broken in February 1971, when Egyptian President Anwar Sadat accepted a proposal by UN mediator Gunnar Jarring, agreeing to full peace with Israel in return for Israeli withdrawal to the prewar Israel-Egypt border. Again, the proposal was pure rejectionism, offering nothing to one of the two contestants for rights in the former Palestine, and in fact was limited to

Israel-Egypt relations. Israel officially welcomed this as a genuine peace offer. In his memoirs, Yitzhak Rabin describes it as a "famous . . . milestone" on the path to peace.

Israel's reaction is reported by Yosi Beilin in his detailed review of internal government records. At a high-level meeting a few days after Sadat's peace offer was received, no one advocated accepting it. Abba Eban proposed a conditional response, with "Israeli armed forces to withdraw from the cease-fire line with Egypt to secure, recognized, and agreed borders which will be established in the peace agreement," not the borders assumed in UN 242 and the Jarring Memorandum. Golda Meir's hawkish adviser Yisrael Galili objected even to this, suggesting instead outright rejection with the formula: "Israel will not withdraw to the pre-June 5 1967 borders." Moshe Dayan and Yitzhak Rabin agreed, and convinced the cabinet to accept Galili's proposal. Jordan had expressed its interest in a settlement through the 1967–1973 period in "direct secret meetings between the highest officials in Jordan and Israel" and in other ways, Beilin alleges, observing also that even Galili "did not deny the possibility for a peace settlement on the June 4, 1967 borders."[44]

Adopting Galili's formula, Israel rejected Sadat's peace offer, preferring expansion to peace. The reasoning was outlined publicly by General (ret.) Haim Bar-Lev of the governing Labor Party:

I think that we could obtain a peace settlement on the basis of the earlier [pre-June 1967] borders. If I were persuaded that this is the maximum that we might obtain, I would say: agreed. But I think that it is not the maximum. I think that if we continue to hold out, we will obtain more.

Ezer Weizman, now president, added that if Israel were to accept UN 242 as interpreted by the United States and other great powers, it could not "exist according to the scale, spirit, and quality she now embodies." Israeli commentator Amos Elon wrote ten years later that Sadat had caused "panic" among the Israeli political leadership when he announced his willingness "to enter into a peace agreement with Israel, and to respect its independence and sovereignty in 'secure and recognized borders.'"[45] As in other cases, the "panic" was overcome by holding fast. Sometimes resorting to violence seemed a better means, as in Lebanon in 1982, when Israel invaded to overcome the threat of PLO moderation, a "veritable catastrophe" for the Israeli government, which invaded in the hope of compelling "the stricken PLO" to "return to its earlier terrorism," thus

"undercutting the danger" of negotiations, historian Yehoshua Po-
rath pointed out shortly after the invasion, a judgement well-
supported on other grounds.[46]

In 1971, Israel chose the near certainty of military confrontation
and terror, not the possibility of diplomatic settlement. One may debate the merits of the choice, but a choice it was. In Bar-Lev's terms
the choice was justified: reliance on force rather than diplomacy did
allow Israel to "obtain more," under the "peace process."

Sadat's peace offer faced Washington with a dilemma. Egypt's
position was in accord with the official U.S. stand; Israel's was not.
An internal debate followed, with the State Department keeping to
the earlier position and National Security Adviser Henry Kissinger
advocating what he called "stalemate": no negotiations or diplomacy, just reliance on force. Kissinger gives reasons in his memoirs,
but they are so outlandish that they can be dismissed (they are generally ignored in the professional literature).[47] Kissinger prevailed,
and soon took over the State Department, eliminating his rival
William Rogers, possibly the real motive in this affair. The United
States, accordingly, changed its interpretation of UN 242 to permit
only partial withdrawal, as the United States and Israel unilaterally
determine. Given U.S. power, that has been the operative meaning
of UN 242 since 1971.

This was a major turning point in Middle East diplomacy, of great
significance today. Since that time, the United States has barred
every diplomatic initiative based on UN 242 under its original
meaning, in complete diplomatic isolation (along with Israel).

U.S.–Israeli isolation became even more extreme by the mid-
1970s, as the international consensus shifted toward recognition of
Palestinian rights, and UN resolutions recognizing those rights
were added to UN 242 in the diplomatic process—not given the
name "peace process" because the world-dominant state opposed
it. The issue reached the Security Council in January 1976, with a
resolution incorporating the language of state alongside Israel. The
resolution was supported by virtually the entire world, including
the major Arab states, the PLO, Europe, the nonaligned countries,
and the Soviet Union, which was in the mainstream of international
diplomacy throughout. According to Israeli UN Ambassador Haim
Herzog, later president, the PLO not only backed the plan but in
fact "prepared it."[48]

Israel refused to attend the UN session. Instead, it bombed
Lebanon once again, killing over fifty villagers in what it called a

"preventive" strike, presumably retaliation against UN diplomacy. By Western standards, such actions do not fall under "the plague of international terrorism."

The United States vetoed the resolution, as it did again in 1980. From the mid-1970s, the United States blocked all initiatives from the UN, Europe, the Arab states, the USSR, and the PLO, with increasing intensity from the early 1980s. Though the Security Council was eliminated by the U.S. veto, the General Assembly continued to pass such resolutions at its annual meetings, with overwhelming support, United States–Israel opposed, as on many other issues. The last such vote was in December 1990, 144 to 2. The date is significant.

Virtually all of this is out of history, ignored or distorted even in scholarly work, and flatly denied in journalism and intellectual discourse. Apparently, the picture of the United States as the leader of the Rejection Front cannot be assimilated into the intellectual culture. Hence, history has been rewritten, a rather impressive achievement, which I have reviewed elsewhere.[49] The facts have been available regularly in marginalized dissident literature, but rarely elsewhere.

More interesting is that the facts seem to have been erased from the memories of Israeli leaders who could not have failed to know them, for example, the generally realistic Moshe Dayan, who, in November 1976, said in a confidential interview that "there is a real hope that Egypt may want peace with us" some day, perhaps even other Arab states. Such reactions may be a symptom of the "panic" Elon described over the threat of a diplomatic settlement, which would undermine the "permanent rule" over the territories that Dayan had anticipated when serving as defense minister in the Labor government, pre-1973.[50]

After the rejection of his 1971 peace offer, Sadat tried in many ways to gain Washington's attention; among other initiatives, he expelled Soviet advisers, thereby "abandoning Egyptian intention to destroy the Zionist reality," Dayan observes in the same interview.[51] Sadat also threatened war if the United States and Israel continued to reject a peaceful settlement. American diplomats in the Middle East, businessmen, and others, urged Kissinger to take these threats seriously, but he dismissed them on the prevailing assumptions about Israeli military dominance: for example, that Israel is a military power on a par with Britain and France and could immediately conquer the area from Khartoum to Baghdad to Algeria if necessary

(General Ariel Sharon) and would "trample Arab faces in the mud" if they forgot the fact of life (Israeli radio), whereas "war is not the Arabs' game."[52]

The 1973 war dispelled these rather racist theses. Kissinger came to realize that Egypt could not simply be disregarded. The next best option was to remove it from the conflict, a policy that culminated in the Camp David agreements of 1978–1979, which left Israel free to integrate the Occupied Territories and attack Lebanon. So it proceeded to do with the Arab deterrent removed. These implications of Camp David were obvious at once, and are now generally acknowledged, for example by Israeli strategic analyst Avner Yaniv, who observes that the effect of the "Egyptian defection" was to "free" Israel "to sustain military operations against the PLO in Lebanon as well as settlement activity on the West Bank." In reality, the military operations regularly targeted Lebanese civilians from the early 1970s, guided by the "rational prospect, ultimately fulfilled, that affected populations would exert pressure for the cessation of hostilities" and acceptance of Israeli arrangements for the region, Abba Eban observed. Eban's advocacy of international terrorism was in response to Prime Minister Begin's account of atrocities in Lebanon committed under the Labor government in the style "of regimes which neither Mr. Begin nor I would dare to mention by name," Eban observed, acknowledging the accuracy of the account.[53]

Sadat's 1977 initiatives were welcomed, turning him into a hero and a "man of peace," and very definitely entering history, though his proposals were far less acceptable to Israel than the suppressed and forgotten "famous milestone" of 1971, because he now called for Palestinian rights, in accord with the revised international consensus. The reason for the different reactions is simple: the 1973 war.

By the late 1980s, U.S.–Israeli extremism was running into difficulties. The Intifada threatened Israel's control of the territories, and by late 1988, Washington was becoming an object of international ridicule for its increasingly desperate efforts not to hear the diplomatic initiatives from the PLO and others. By December, Secretary of State George Shultz gave up the game. Washington grudgingly "declared victory," announcing that the PLO had capitulated and uttered the "magic words"—namely, reiterating its unchanged position, which Washington could no longer ignore. The preferred version is the one that Shultz reports in his memoirs: before, Arafat had been saying in one place "'Unc, unc, unc,' and in another he was saying 'cle, cle, cle,' but nowhere will he yet bring himself to say 'Uncle,'" in the style of abject surrender of "insignificant people."

Washington announced further that as a reward for its sudden good behavior, the PLO would be permitted to have a "dialogue" with the United States, plainly a delaying tactic. The protocols of the first meeting were leaked and published in Egypt and in Israel, there, with much jubilation over the fact that "the American representative adopted the Israeli positions." U.S. Ambassador Robert Pelletreau stated two preconditions that the PLO must accept for the dialogue to proceed: it must abandon the idea of an international conference, and call off the "riots" in the Occupied Territories (the Intifada), "which we view as terrorist acts against Israel." In short, the PLO must ensure a return to the pre-Intifada status quo, so that Israel would be able to continue its expansion and repression in the territories with United States support.

The ban on an international conference follows from the unwillingness of the world to adopt U.S. rejectionism at that time. As Henry Kissinger had privately explained, his diplomatic efforts were designed "to ensure that the Europeans and Japanese did not get involved in the diplomacy concerning the Middle East" (also "to isolate the Palestinians" so that they would not be a factor in the outcome, and "to break up the Arab united front," thus allowing Israel "to deal separately with each of its neighbors").[54]

The background for Pelletreau's second precondition is made clear in another UN resolution barred by the United States: the 1987 General Assembly resolution condemning "Terrorism Wherever and by Whomever Committed." The offending clause is

that nothing in the present resolution could in any way prejudice the right to self-determination, freedom and independence, as derived from the Charter of the United Nations, of peoples forcibly deprived of that right . . . , particularly peoples under colonial and racist regimes and foreign occupation or other forms of colonial domination, nor . . . the right of these peoples to struggle to this end and to seek and receive support [in accordance with the Charter and other principles of international law].

These rights are not accepted by the United States, Israel, or at the time, their South African ally. The resolution passed, 153 to 2, the United States and Israel opposed, Honduras alone abstaining. It was therefore effectively vetoed (also unreported and banned from history). For similar reasons, the United States rejected the declaration of the 1993 Vienna Conference on Human Rights that "any foreign occupation is a human rights violation," also unreported.[55]

On these assumptions, protests in the Occupied Territories are "terrorism against the State of Israel."

In February 1989, Yitzhak Rabin had a meeting with Peace Now leaders in which he expressed his satisfaction with the U.S.–PLO dialogue, which he described as "low-level discussions" that avoid any serious issue and grant Israel "at least a year" to resolve the problem by force. "The inhabitants of the territories are subject to harsh military and economic pressure," Rabin explained, and "In the end, they will be broken," and will accept Israel's terms.[56]

These terms were spelled out in the May 1989 plan of the Peres-Shamir coalition government, which stipulated that there can be no "additional Palestinian state" (Jordan already being a "Palestinian state"), and that "There will be no change in the status of Judea, Samaria and Gaza other than in accordance with the basic guidelines of the [Israeli] Government." Furthermore, Israel would conduct no negotiations with the PLO, though it would permit "free elections," to be conducted under Israeli military rule with much of the Palestinian leadership in prison without charge or expelled.

This proposal was praised for its "great promise and potential" by prominent American doves (Aaron David Miller of the State Department, Middle East commentator Helena Cobban), who mentioned only that Israel might allow "free elections." In December 1989, the State Department's James Baker plan officially endorsed the Peres-Shamir plan, offering Palestinians a dialogue on measures to implement it; no other issues were to be raised.

Again, the essential facts have yet to reach the American public, except at the margins.

There remained the problem of how to implement the extreme form of rejectionism advocated by the Labor-Likud coalition and the Bush administration, as by their predecessors. That problem was solved a few months later, when Saddam Hussein invaded Kuwait, having misunderstood the rules of world order, as dictators are prone to do in their isolation. Bush continued to send aid to Saddam until the day of the invasion, as did Thatcher, and the State Department indicated to him that Washington would not object if he were to rectify a disputed border with Kuwait and shake his fist at other oil producers to induce them to raise prices. Saddam perhaps interpreted this as authorization to take over Kuwait. At that point, the principles enunciated in 1958 came into force.

The Bush administration feared that Saddam would immediately withdraw, leaving a puppet regime in place; that is, that he would duplicate what the United States had just done in Panama. No historical parallel is exact, of course. Civilian casualties in Panama were apparently higher than in Kuwait at that stage, and there were other differences. In internal discussions, chairman of the Joint Chiefs Colin Powell warned that in "The next few days Iraq will withdraw," putting "his puppet in, [and] Everyone in the Arab world will be happy."[57] Latin Americans, in contrast, were anything but happy about similar U.S. actions in Panama. But the major difference is that as the global superpower, the United States could veto Security Council resolutions and nullify other objections to its invasion of Panama and could mobilize rather unwilling international support to ensure that apparent Iraqi withdrawal initiatives would be dismissed and that the reaction would be "ruthless," as prescribed years earlier. An instructive series of events followed, reviewed elsewhere.[58]

As bombs and missiles were falling on Baghdad and peasant recruits hiding in the sands, George Bush announced the basic principle of the New World Order in four simple words: "What We Say Goes." What "we say" was made crystal clear as the shooting stopped. Immediately, a rebellion in the Shi'ite regions of southern Iraq sought to overthrow Saddam, who launched a vicious counterattack. The United States stood by quietly, refusing even to allow rebelling Iraqi generals access to captured Iraqi military equipment to protect the population from Saddam's slaughter. The official reasoning was outlined by Thomas Friedman, chief diplomatic correspondent of the *New York Times*: "The best of all worlds" for Washington, he explained, would be "an iron-fisted Iraqi junta without Saddam Hussein," a return to the happy days when Saddam's "iron fist . . . held Iraq together, much to the satisfaction of the American allies Turkey and Saudi Arabia"—and, of course, their superpower patron. But since no suitable clone could be found, it would be necessary to settle for second best: an iron-fisted junta run by the Beast of Baghdad himself. U.S.–UK policy was described by the Chairman of the House of Commons Foreign Affairs Committee, David Howell, as saying to Saddam, "It is all right now, you are free to commit any atrocities you like."

U.S. officials confirmed that the Bush administration would persist in their refusal to talk to Iraqi democrats or to raise questions about democracy in Kuwait. That would be inappropriate interference in the internal affairs of other countries, they explained. For Iraq, what matters is "stability," and that meant support for Saddam as he crushed the southern rebellion under the eyes of Stormin' Norman Schwarzkopf, and then turned to the north to crush the Kurdish uprising. In the latter case, an unanticipated popular reaction in the West forced Washington to put some limits on Saddam's atrocities, though he did receive vocal support from Turkey, brutally repressing its own Kurdish population, and from Israel, where military and political figures (including the retiring chief of staff and leading doves) warned that Kurdish autonomy might create a territorial link between Damascus and Teheran, so that the butcher should be allowed to carry out his necessary work. Turkish concerns received some mention in the United States, but not the Israeli reaction, which clashed too sharply with preferred imagery.[59]

The aftermath of the Gulf War offered both a need and an opportunity for the United States to implement its rejectionist program. The need arose from the ugly picture in the Gulf region: the Beast of Baghdad back in charge, now with tacit rather than overt U.S. support as before; the uprisings violently crushed; the Arab Facade safeguarded from democratic pressures; and reports beginning to come in from respected Western medical sources and human rights groups about thousands of Iraqi children dying from sanctions that were aimed at the civilian population, not Saddam. That was not a scene to be left in public memory, particularly after the jingoist frenzy and awe for the Grand Leader that had been whipped up by the doctrinal system. A triumph was badly needed.

The opportunity arose from the fact that the world now accepted the guiding principle of the New World Order: "What We Say Goes," at least in the Middle East. Europe backed away. Its only further role was to facilitate U.S. rejectionist programs, as Norway did in 1993. The Soviet Union was gone. The Third World was in disarray, in part as a result of the economic catastrophe of the 1980s. The United States was at last free to implement the two basic principles it had upheld in isolation for twenty years: (1) No international conference, though the Russians were allowed in as a fig leaf; (2) No right of self-determination for the Palestinians.

That was the framework of the Madrid negotiations, which began in Fall 1991 to great fanfare and applause. Negotiations dragged on while Israel continued its expansion into the territories with U.S. support, though Washington continued to prefer the style of Labor, which understands better than Likud how to present its actions so that they will be accepted rather than condemned. In other respects the differences are not great. The Clinton administration came as something of a surprise in its support for more extreme Israeli policies. There were also increasing challenges to Arafat within the Palestinian community, reported in Israel through the summer of 1993, also from Jordan and Lebanon.

In September 1993, the Declaration of Principles was signed in Washington. It incorporated the basic principles of U.S.–Israeli rejectionism. First, the "permanent status" is to be based solely on UN 242, which offers nothing to the Palestinians, not on 242 *and other relevant UN resolutions* that the United States has barred since the mid-1970s because they recognize Palestinian rights. Second, UN 242 is to be understood in the terms unilaterally imposed by the U.S. since 1971 (meaning partial withdrawal) and incorporated in the Peres-Shamir-Baker plan of 1989. Presumably, the United States and Israel modify that plan at least rhetorically. It would make sense for them to use the term "state" to refer to whatever scattered cantons they decide to leave to local Palestinian administration, much as South Africa did when it established the "homelands" in the early 1960s—a program that merited the term "peace process" as much as the present one does, but did not gain that status because it was not an expression of the rules of world order that are established by the powerful.

Whether the United States and Israel decide to call the cantons a "state" or something else—perhaps "fried chicken" as David Bar-Ilan elegantly suggested[60]—the results are likely to resemble the Bantustan model. No one familiar with the situation in the territories created by the Rabin-Peres-Netanyahu governments and their predecessors will fail to recognize the picture given in a standard work of African history:

South African retention of effective power through its officials in the Bantustans, its overwhelming economic influence and security arrangements gave to this initiative [of elections] elements of a farce. However, unlikely candidates as were the Bantustans for any meaningful independent existence, their expanding bureaucracies provided jobs for new strata of educated Africans tied to the system in a new way and a basis of accumulation for a small number of Africans with access to loans and political influence. Repression, too, could be indigenised through developing homeland policy and army personnel. On the fringe of the Bantustans, border industry growth centres were planned as a means of freeing capital from some of the restraints that influx control imposed on industrial expansion elsewhere and to take advantage of virtually captive and particularly cheap labour. Within the homelands economic development was more a matter of advertising brochures than actual practical activity although some officials in South Africa understood the needs from their own perspective for some kind of revitalisation of the homelands to prevent their economies from collapsing further.[61]

So far, Israeli officials have not recognized any need to keep the economies of the cantons from collapsing even further, though sooner or later they may see the merit in the demands of Israeli industrialists for a "transition from colonialism to neo-colonialism" in the territories with the collaboration of "the representatives of the Palestinian bourgeoisie," thus creating "a situation similar to the relations between France and many of its former colonies in Africa"— or the United States and Mexico, Western investors and the Third World that is being restored in Eastern Europe, or international capital in southeast China, etc.

As in the United States, the threat to transfer production across the border can be used effectively to undermine unions, lower wages, increase inequality, and diminish the threat of democracy. "If any union even thinks of striking, the manufacturers can close their factories and set up new ones in Gaza," Histadrut officers explain, a prospect that was particularly appealing to Yitzhak Rabin, who had "never concealed his animosity toward the Histadrut or his free-market leanings"—"free market" U.S.-style, with the economy based on massive state subsidy for wealth and privilege and spin-offs from military industry. A model is suggested by recent events in Ofakim, where a factory was closed shortly after its owners received a substantial public subsidy and transferred across the border to enjoy much cheaper labor with few benefits, a good illustration of the promise of the Peres's "new order" in the Middle East.[62]

For the time being, however, Israeli policies continue to contribute to the further collapse of the economies. The territories were not permitted to develop under Israeli rule and are now spinning rapidly downward, though Palestinians "tied to the system" and "with access to loans and political influence" can enrich themselves by robbing foreign aid with Israel's cooperation. Similarly, the United States winks at Israel's rampant corruption, for example, the diversion of billions of dollars of U.S. loan guarantees, theoretically for immigrants, to give "Israel's banking system (taken over by the government after the bank shares scandal) greater liquidity and willingness to extend credit to corporations, small businesses, and private individuals," enabling Israelis to "purchase automobiles, foreign travel, or speculate on the stock market" in an artificially rich country that is now competing with its sponsor for the lead in inequality in the industrial world. Widespread corruption in client states is considered no more of a problem than at home, as long as the "significant people" are receiving their due.[63]

The IMF reported that through 1996, unemployment nearly doubled in the Occupied Territories since the Oslo process began and per capita income shrank 20 percent, while investment halved. The further devastation of the economy results in part from the closures, which were particularly harsh under Labor, and from Israel's policy of blocking Palestinian exports while maintaining a captive market for expensive Israeli imports, made even more costly as they pass through the monopolies established as payoffs by the Palestinian Authority. Meanwhile, the IMF reports, total Israeli exports grew by almost half, "nearly doubling in Asian markets opened up by the peace process, while foreign investment in Israel went up sixfold." The UN agencies in the territories estimate the decline in per capita GNP since Oslo I to be about 40 percent, accelerating "the retardation of development in the territories that began in 1967." Other informed observers give still higher estimates of the decline.

In short, the "peace process" follows a rule of very great generality: it serves the interests of its architects quite nicely, while the interests of others are "an incident, not an end." As for the "insignificant people," the "peace process" has offered the United States and Israel new mechanisms to follow the advice of Moshe Dayan, one of the Labor leaders more sympathetic to the Palestinian plight, in the early days of the occupation: Israel should tell the Palestinian refugees in the territories that "we have no solution, you shall continue to live like dogs, and whoever wishes may leave, and we will see where this process leads." The suggestion is natural within the overriding conception articulated by Haim Herzog in 1972: "I do not deny the Palestinians a place or stand or opinion on every matter. . . . But certainly I am not prepared to consider them as partners in any respect in a land that has been consecrated in the hands of our nation for thousands of years. For the Jews of this land there cannot be any partner."[64]

Nothing fundamental has changed in the conception of the Labor doves and their U.S. sponsors, apart from new modalities.

At the peak period of Israeli rejectionism in mid-1988, Yitzhak Rabin called for a settlement leaving Israel in control of 40 percent of the West Bank and Gaza, an updated version of the Allon Plan. At Oslo II, he agreed to accept twice that much, though surely Israel will want to transfer more mostly useless land to local Palestinian administration, while keeping control of the resources and valuable sectors, perhaps reaching Rabin's 1988 figure.

After Oslo II, Peres informed a gathering of ambassadors in Jerusalem that "this solution about which everyone is thinking and which is what you want will never happen." He continued to act resolutely to ensure that outcome with U.S. funding and support—for example, in February 1996, when his housing minister, Binyamin ("Fuad") Ben-Eliezer, announced the construction of 6,500 units for Jews only in the area of southeast Jerusalem that Israel calls "Har Homa," with groundbreaking scheduled to begin in a year, just when it took place, though now under Likud. Only a few days before Netanyahu was elected, dozens of Palestinians tried to block Peres's bulldozers paving the way to the planned settlement at Har Homa. Ben-Eliezer also announced other building plans that appear to be more significant, particularly those to the east of Jerusalem (Plan E-1). These developments will effectively split the West Bank into two cantons when Ma'ale Adumim is incorporated into "Greater Jerusalem" in accord with the plans announced and implemented by the Rabin–Peres administrations after the Oslo agreements and now pursued by their Likud successor. While attention was focused on the Har Homa/Jabal Abu Ghneim constructions, falsely attributed to Likud initiatives, Defense Minister Yitzhak Mordechai announced that Labor's E-1 program would be implemented, with new housing construction and road building. MK Michael Kleiner, the head of the expansionist "Land of Israel Front" (Hazit Erez Yisrael), greeted the announcement with appreciation, observing that this plan, which "was the initiative of the former Housing Minister Binyamin Ben-Eliezer with the authorization of Yitzhak Rabin," is "the most important" of the Front's demands, more so than Har Homa.

Ben-Eliezer also explained that "Fuad does everything quietly, with the complete protection of the Prime Minister," using such terms as "natural growth" instead of "new settlements" when he implements Labor's policies of expanding Greater Jerusalem to include Ma'ale Adumim, Givat Ze'ev, and Beitar as the "first circle" of settlements surrounding Jerusalem, to which another "chain of settlements" is to be added in a second circle. According to Labor dove Yosi Beilin, the Rabin government "increased settlements by 50 percent in Judea and Samaria (the West Bank) after Oslo," but "we did it quietly and with wisdom," whereas you, Netanyahu, "proclaim your intentions every morning, frighten the Palestinians and transform the topic of Jerusalem as the unified capital of Israel—a matter which all Israelis agree upon—into a subject of world-wide debate." The statement is only partially accurate, since the "quiet wisdom" extends well beyond Jerusalem.[65]

The difference of style can presumably be traced to the constituencies of the two political groups. Labor, the party of educated professionals and westernized elites, is more attuned to Western norms and understands that the sponsors should be offered a way "not to see" what they are doing. Likud's brazen and crude methods of achieving basically the same results are an embarrassment to Western humanists, and sometimes lead to conflict and annoyance.

The Labor/Likud program of establishing a Bantustan-style settlement cannot be accused of violating the "peace process." Oslo I says nothing relevant, apart from the stipulations about the "permanent status" already mentioned, which establish the basic principles of the Peres-Shamir-Baker plan and long-term U.S.–Israeli rejectionism. Oslo II, in contrast, is quite explicit about many important topics. I have reviewed the details elsewhere and will not repeat.[66] In brief, it grants Israel permanent control over most of the crucial water resources and imposes purposefully humiliating conditions on Palestinians, even with regard to such matters as transit of Palestinian police on "Palestinian roads." These abominations are designed to make life for Palestinians as miserable as possible while Israelis and tourists speed to their destinations on the modern "bypass" highways that free them from the need to see the Arab population who are to survive somehow, isolated from their families, workplaces, and institutions. With regard to land, the agreement allows Israel to do virtually what it likes. Oslo II even states that Palestinians "shall respect the legal rights of Israelis (including corporations owned by Israelis) related to lands located in areas under the territorial jurisdiction of the [Palestinian] Council"—that is, the whole of the Occupied Territories—specifically, their rights related to government and absentee land, an indefinite category that expands at Israel's whim, reaching perhaps 70 percent of the territories, according to the Israeli press.[67] Oslo II thus abrogates the stand of the entire world, including technically the United States, that legal rights cannot be attained by conquest, and rescinds even the post-1971 U.S. interpretation of UN 242.

Palestinians and others are only deluding themselves and others when they say that Israel committed itself to "withdraw from occupied Palestinian territories, including Jerusalem," in accord with UN 242, or anything remotely like it; or that they agreed to grant Palestinians "control over water, telecommunications and transport, among other things"; or that George Bush's Madrid initiative "involved the implementation of UN Security Council resolutions on Palestine" (Palestinian Foreign Minister Farouk Kadoumi); or that "the terms of reference" for the "peace process" are given by UN 242, the Oslo Accords, and the Madrid Conference, "which enshrine the land-for-peace principle" (Egyptian diplomat Abdelaleem El-Abayad).[68] Nothing of the sort is true, as the documents make clear and the consistent practice even more so, unless we interpret such phrases as "land-for-peace" with the cynicism that would have welcomed the South African homelands policy.

Israeli doves may prefer what some observers have called a state of "collective self-denial," avoiding the documents and the historical context that gives them meaning, perhaps even "not seeing" what is happening a few miles from where they live—not a phenomenon unique to Israel, needless to say. The funders and supporters elsewhere may also find the stance convenient. But the realities remain.

The realities go beyond the Occupied Territories, including also Israel within the Green Line, where South African analogies are again unfortunately not inappropriate, if by no means exact. And crucially, they extend to the Palestinian diaspora, particularly now that Clinton has broken with official U.S. policy since 1948 and now (alone with Israel) rejects UN resolution 194 of December 11, 1948, which spells out the concrete meaning of Article 13 of the UN Universal Declaration of Human Rights, adopted on December 10, 1948. Since a negative U.S. vote is effectively a veto, the right of Palestinians to return or receive compensation is thereby formally abrogated. The endorsement was always hypocritical. There was no intention of implementing resolution 194, even the right to compensation, which Israeli Foreign Minister Moshe Sharett estimated at $1 billion current dollar value even without interest.[69]

If current plans succeed, the predictions of Israeli government Arabists in 1948 might be fulfilled: the refugees would either assimilate elsewhere or "would be crushed" and "die," while "most of them would turn into human dust and the waste of society, and join the most impoverished classes in the Arab countries."[70] Apart from privileged sectors that accommodate to the "neo-colonial" settlement, those remaining in the territories can look forward to the bright future of Haitians toiling in U.S. assembly plants for a few cents an hour or the semi-slave laborers in China's foreign-controlled export industries. And Palestinians within Israel may expect to live as American Jews and Blacks would if the United States were to become "the sovereign State of Christian Whites" throughout the world (to paraphrase Israeli law), not the state of its citizens.

Such consequences need not come to pass, but they might, and if they do, privileged sectors of American, Israeli, and Palestinian society will have a lot to answer for, in my opinion.

NOTES

1. I have written about these matters often since the June 1967 War, most recently in *World Orders, Old and New* (New York: Columbia University Press, 1994); extended in 1996 with an Epilogue carrying the account through Oslo II, the 1996 Israeli attack on Lebanon, and the May 1996 Israeli elections. Sources not cited in text can be found in *World Orders, Old and New*.

2. In 1995, Venezuela edged out Saudi Arabia for the first time since the 1970s, Allanna Sullivan, *Wall Street Journal*, 3 January 1996. On U.S.–Venezuela relations, which go well beyond iron, see Stephen Rabe, *The Road to OPEC* (Austin: University of Texas Press, 1982).

3. For production data, see David Painter, *Oil and the American Century* (Baltimore: Johns Hopkins University Press, 1986), 218. In 1925, the United States produced over 71 percent of the world's oil, the Caribbean 14 percent. In 1965, the U.S. share was over 27 percent, almost twice that of the next producer, USSR, Venezuela was third.

4. Rabe, *The Road to OPEC*; Lansing-Wilson cited by Gabriel Kolko, *Main Currents in American History* (New York: Pantheon, 1984), 47.

5. August, March 1945; William Roger Louis, *The British Empire in the Middle East: 1945–1951* (Oxford: Oxford University Press, 1984), 231, 191. For recent reviews of U.S. policies in the region, with special focus on Lebanon (important in large part as a transit point for oil), see Irene Gendzier, *Notes from the Minefield* (New York: Columbia University Press, 1997).

6. David Sanger, *New York Times*, 21 February 1997.

7. Jules Kagian, *Middle East International*, 21 October 1994.

8. Gerald Haines, *The Americanization of Brazil* (Wilmington, DE: Scholarly Resources, 1989); Gendzier, *Notes from the Minefield*, 41, citing treasurer Leo Welch.

9. *Fortune,* January 1948. The specific reference is to the aircraft industry, today the leading "civilian" exporter thanks to massive public subsidy over the years, but it was recognized that this is a model for "the future shape of the US economy" quite generally. For more on the matter, see Chomsky, *World Orders, Old and New,* chapter 2.

10. The first extensive work on the topic, still unequalled, is Gabriel Kolko, *Politics of War* (New York: Random House, 1968). For a general review using more recent sources as well, see my *Deterring Democracy* (London: Verso, 1991; extended 1992 [Vintage, Hill and Wang]), chapter 11.

11. *Foreign Relations of the United States (FRUS),*1948, III, NSC 1/3, March 8, 1948, 775f.; Kennan, 848f. See 1945 review cited by Michael Leffler, *A Preponderance of Power* (Stanford: Stanford University Press, 1992), 71.

12. For ample illustration, see Edward Herman, *The Real Terror Network* (Boston: South End Press, 1982); my *Pirates and Emperors* (New York: Claremont, 1986 [Amana, Pluto, Black Rose]); Alexander George, ed., *Western State Terrorism* (London: Polity, 1991). Oil companies and Italy, John Blair, *Control of Oil* (New York: Pantheon, 1976), 94f.

13. Gendzier, *Notes from the Minefield,* 24f; Robert McMahon, *The Cold War on the Periphery* (New York: Columbia University Press, 1994), 221.

14. From State Department records, expressing concerns over the "philosophy of the new nationalism" sweeping Latin America, safely interred at a February 1945 hemispheric conference where the United States imposed its Economic Charter of the Americas that guaranteed an end to economic nationalism "in all its forms." See David Green, *The Containment of Latin America* (New York: Quadrangle, 1971), VII.2. For many examples, including these, see my *Year 501* (Boston: South End Press, 1993), chapters 2, 7, and sources cited.

15. *Central America Report* (Guatemala), February 4, 1994. See *Deterring Democracy,* chapters 5, 6.

16. In the United States, this is invariably termed humanitarian aid, another expression of the disdain of the intellectual culture for international law when it interferes with state violence. The explicit determination of the World Court that all such aid was military, not humanitarian, was considered unworthy of report.

17. *Deterring Democracy,* chapters 5, 6.

18. The United States has been far in the lead in vetoing Security Council resolutions since the UN fell out of control with decolonization; the UK is second, France a distant third. For fact and propaganda on these matters, see Ibid., chapter 6.5.

19. Ibid., chapters 1, 3, 5, 6, afterword.

20. *National Security Strategy of the United States, the White House, March 1990.* See Chomsky, *Deterring Democracy,* chapter 1, for excerpts.

21. For a particularly clear acknowledgment, see Christopher Layne (Cato Institute) and Benjamin Schwarz (Rand), *Foreign Policy* (fall 1993).

22. Frank Costigliola, in Thomas Peterson, ed., *Kennedy's Quest for Victory* (Oxford: Oxford University Press, 1989); the reference is presumably to Dean Acheson.

23. John Balfour, British Embassy in Washington, to Bevin, August 9, 1945; Bevin, November 8, 1945. Cited by Mark Curtis, *Ambiguities of Power* (London: Zed, 1995), 18, 23.

24. Christopher Thorne, *The Issue of War* (Oxford: Oxford University Press, 1985), 225, 211. On the contempt for England and Europe generally, see Frank Costigliola, "Kennedy and the Failure to Consult," *Political Science Quarterly* (spring 1995).

25. William Stivers, *Supremacy and Oil* (Ithaca: Cornell University Press, 1982), 28, 34; *America's Confrontation with Revolutionary Change in the Middle East* (New York: St. Martin's, 1986), 20f; 1946, Louis, *The British Empire in the Middle East: 1945–1951*, 353.

26. Diane Kunz, *Butter and Guns: America's Cold War Economic Diplomacy* (New York: Free Press, 1997), 226, 88; Nadav Safran, *Israel: The Embattled Ally* (Cambridge, MA: Harvard University Press, 1978), 576, 110. Under Carter, U.S. aid to Israel rose to about half of total aid. Increasingly over the years, the official figures are greatly underestimated because of failure to include prepayment, forgiven loans, and other devices.

27. See my article in *Le Monde diplomatique* (April 1977), reprinted in *Towards a New Cold War* (New York: Pantheon, 1982), chapter 11.

28. Keegan quoted by Richard Hudson, *Wall Street Journal*, 5 February 1991; Lloyd George quoted in V. G. Kiernan, *European Empires from Conquest to Collapse* (London: Fontana, 1982), 200. On Churchill's enthusiasm for the use of "poisoned gas against uncivilised tribes" (specifically Kurds and Afghans, but "recalcitrant Arabs" generally), see Andy Thomas, *Effects of Chemical Warfare* (Stockholm International Peace Research Institute [SIPRI], London: Taylor and Francis, 1985), chapter 2. For quotes, see my *Turning the Tide* (Boston: South End Press, 1985), 126; *Deterring Democracy*, chapter 6.1.

29. Irving Kristol, *Wall Street Journal*, 13 December 1973; Walter Laqueur, *New York Times Magazine*, 16 December 1973; reference to wheat prices, Emma Rothschild, ibid., 13 March 1977; Ruth Wisse, *Commentary* (May 1988); Janet Tassel, "Mame-Loshn at Harvard," *Harvard Magazine* (July/August 1997); Martin Peretz, Interview in *Ha'aretz*, 4 June 1982.

30. For a broader sample, see my *Necessary Illusions* (Boston: South End Press, 1989), 315f.

31. Daniel B. Schirmer, *Fidel Ramos—the Pentagon's Philippine Friend 1992–1997* (Cambridge, MA: Friends of the Filipino People, 1997).

32. Robert Komer cited by Melvyn Leffler, *Diplomatic History*, vol. 7, 1983, 245f; Dulles/Eisenhower cited by Irwin Wall, *Diplomatic History*, Fall 1994, from the Eisenhower Library, *Foreign Relations of the United States (FRUS)* 1958–1990, XVII, *Indonesia* (Washington, 1994), April 8 and August

12, 1958; quotes are from U.S.–Jakarta Embassy cables, reporting Indonesian government conclusions, endorsed by the Joint Chiefs of Staff the same day. On Indonesia, see my *Powers and Prospects* (Boston: South End Press, 1996), chapter 7, and sources cited; and on the reaction to the slaughter, *Year 501*, chapter 5. North African policy, *Foreign Relations of the United States (FRUS)*, 1947, V, 688, cited by Mark Curtis, *Ambiguities of Power*, 21. On the Middle East at the time, see particularly Gendzier, *Notes from the Minefield*.

33. Kunz, *Butter and Guns*, 237.

34. Albert Cavallo, "What Price Oil," in *Proceedings, 17th Annual Wind Energy Conference, July 1995* (London: Mechanical Engineering Publications, 1995).

35. Wilbur Edel, "Diplomatic History—State Department Style," *Political Science Quarterly*, 106, no. 4 (1991–1992).

36. For further elaboration, quotes, and sources on what follows, see Chomsky, *Deterring Democracy*, chapter 6; also *World Orders, Old and New*, chapter 3; Gendzier, *Notes from the Minefield*.

37. On Southeast Asia, see my *For Reasons of State* (New York: Pantheon, 1973), chapter 1.V; *Rethinking Camelot* (Boston: South End Press, 1993). For Latin America the point is obvious. Britain's analysis was much the same, throughout the Third World. See Curtis, *Ambiguities of Power*.

38. The statement continues: "the demise of the Soviet Union left the United States as the single power broker in the region and as such interested in its stability and prosperity." The United States is indeed interested in the "stability" of the region, in the technical sense of the term (meaning, subordination to U.S. power), but is no more interested in its "prosperity" than its European predecessors, as policy demonstrates beyond serious doubt. Boaz Evron, *Jewish State or Israel Nation?* (Bloomington: Indiana University Press, 1995), introduction.

39. *Yediot Ahronot*, April 1992, cited by Israel Shahak, *Middle East International*, 19 March 1993.

40. For some discussion, see my *Fateful Triangle* (Boston: South End Press, 1983).

41. Ibid., 457f. On the aftermath, see John Marshall, Peter Dale Scott, and Jane Hunter, *The Iran-Contra Connection* (Boston: South End Press, 1987) and my *Culture of Terrorism* (Boston: South End Press, 1988). Note that there were no hostages when the arms sales to Iran via Israel began, so it cannot have been an "arms for hostage" deal, as the affair is conventionally interpreted, picking it up at a later stage. Arming the military is a standard device for overthrowing a government, often successful, as in Sukarno's Indonesia and Allende's Chile, to mention two cases that might have been a model for the Iran operation.

42. See the testimony of Assistant Secretary of Defense Edward Gnehm, March 1, 1989, to House Subcommittee on Europe and the Middle East;

Dore Gold, press briefing, Jerusalem, March 9, 1989; Gold, *America, the Gulf, and Israel* (Boulder, CO: Westview, 1988). Reported in Media Analysis Center, *Backgrounder* no. 255 (Jerusalem: March 1989). Gnehm testified that over half of the U.S. Foreign Weapons Evaluation budget was devoted to Israeli products, designed and developed in cooperation with U.S. military industry.

43. For specific details and references, see sources already cited; see also Naseer Aruri, *The Obstruction of Peace* (Monroe, ME: Common Courage, 1995); Norman Finkelstein, *Image and Reality in the Israel-Palestine Conflict* (London: Verso, 1995); Donald Neff, *Fallen Pillars* (Washington, DC: Institute for Palestine Studies, 1995), among others.

44. John Norton Moore, ed., *The Arab-Israeli Conflict*, vol. 3 (Princeton: Princeton University Press, 1974), 1103–11; *The Rabin Memoirs* (New York: Little, Brown, 1979), 192f; Yossi Beilin, *Mehiro shel Ihud* (Revivim, 1985), 118f., 155.

45. Haim Bar-Lev, *Ot*, March 9, 1972, cited by Amnon Kapeliouk, *Le monde diplomatique* (October 1977); Ezer Weizman, *Ha'aretz*, 29 March 1972, cited by John Cooley, *Green March, Black September* (London: Frank Cass, 1973), 162; Amos Elon, *Ha'aretz*, 13 November 1981; the occasion was the "emotional and angry" reaction of the government to the Saudi peace plan of 1981, which "threatened Israel's very existence," Labor Party chairman Shimon Peres wrote in *Ha'aretz*, 10 August 1981, by calling for a diplomatic settlement. In the *New York Times*, criticizing Arab intellectuals for lack of support for the "peace process," Elon wrote that Sadat "was not yet ready to make peace" with Israel in 1972 and attacked the "defeatists" who called for a settlement; *New York Times Magazine*, 11 May 1997.

46. See *Fateful Triangle, Pirates and Emperors;* Norman Finkelstein, *Image and Reality in the Israel-Palestine Conflict.* For a brief review, *World Orders*, chapter 2.

47. For a rare discussion, see my review of Kissinger's memoirs, reprinted in *Towards a New Cold War;* see also David Korn, *Stalemate* (Boulder, CO: Westview, 1992).

48. The PLO representative at the UN condemned the United States for blocking this two-state plan. See *Towards a New Cold War*, 430; Haim Herzog, *Jerusalem Post*, 13 November 1981. The PLO gives the impression that it is unaware of its public support for the resolution. Spokespersons give various versions of the PLO positions over the years, many not very credible.

49. *Towards a New Cold War*, chapter 12; *Fateful Triangle*, chapter 3, particularly notes 88, 111; *Necessary Illusions*, App. 5.4; *Powers and Prospects*, chapter 7.

50. Rami Tal, "Moshe Dayan, Heshbon Nefesh," *Yediot Ahronot*, 27 April 1997, interview of November 22, 1976. See also note 45. Dayan, Kapeliouk, *Le monde diplomatique*, 29, 279; Beilin, *Mehiro shel Ihud*.

51. Along with other analysts, Dayan recognized that Sadat's intentions in the 1973 war were more limited, but seems not to see the implications: that Sadat's actions were an attempt to initiate the diplomatic track that the United States and Israel had blocked.

52. Ariel Sharon, *Yediot Ahronot*, 26 July 1973; Israeli Radio, Joseph Fitchett, *Christian Science Monitor*, 27 October 1973. "Arabs' game," in Amnon Kapeliouk, *Israel: la fin des mythes* (Paris: Albin Michel, 1975), 200f., 281, a conception he attributes to the "General-Professor Yehoshafat Harkabi," a Hebrew University Arabist and former head of military intelligence, later a leading dove. Kapeliouk gives many similar quotes from high-ranking military officers and political leaders. See also my *Peace in the Middle East?* (New York: Pantheon, 1974), chapter 4.

53. *Jerusalem Post*, 16 August 1981; Avner Yaniv, *Dilemmas of Security* (Oxford: Oxford University Press, 1987), 70.

54. Meeting with Jewish leaders, released under the Freedom of Information Act, *MERIP Reports* (May 1981); *Journal of Palestinian Studies* (spring 1981); see *Towards a New Cold War*, 457.

55. UN press release GA/7603, Dec. 7, 1987; see my "International Terrorism: Image and Reality," in George, *Western State Terrorism;* Assistant Secretary of State for Human Rights John Shattuck, cited by Joseph Wronks, *American Society of International Law: Interest Group of the U.N. Decade of International Law*, no. 13 (February 1997).

56. Nahum Barnea, *Yediot Ahronot*, 24 February 1989.

57. Military correspondents Michael Gordon and Gen. (Marines, retired) Bernard Trainor, *New York Times*, 23 October 1994.

58. See *Deterring Democracy*, chapter 6, afterword; Hamid Mowlana, George Gerbner, and Herbert Schiller, *Triumph of the Image* (Boulder, CO: Westview, 1992); Curtis, *Ambiguities of Power.* The best general study is Dilip Hiro, *Desert Shield to Desert Storm* (New York: HarperCollins, 1992), another is Lawrence Freedman and Efraim Karsh, *The Gulf Conflict 1990–1991* (Princeton: Princeton University Press, 1992). Freedman and Karsh praise themselves for "the scope and originality of our analysis," which uses "evidence from *all* available sources," contrasting their achievement with mere journalism. In reality, they ignore entirely or omit basic sources on major issues (for example, prewar diplomatic interactions, which, furthermore, they misrepresent in their scanty comments; the views of the Iraqi democrats and the population of the region generally; the illuminating record of United States and British documents; etc.). Even their efforts to present the United States–United Kingdom effort in the most favorable light conclude that Saddam's goal was not annexation or a "permanent military presence," but "to establish hegemony over Kuwait, ensuring its complete financial, political, and strategic subservience to his wishes," much as intended by the United States in Panama and Israel in Lebanon (and achieved, in the former case). Sad-

dam's scheme "turned sour," they say, because of the international reaction; to translate, because of the differential United States reaction. The authors seem not to realize that their conclusions undercut the central thesis of their book about the nobility of the United States–United Kingdom leadership.

59. Thomas Friedman, *New York Times,* 7 July 1991. For review and sources, see *Deterring Democracy,* chapter 6, afterword; *World Orders,* chapter 1; *Powers and Prospects,* chapter 7; David Howell, cited by Mark Curtis, "Obstacles to Security in the Middle East" in *Prospects for Global Order,* vol. 2, edited by Seizaburo Sato and Trevor Taylor (London: Royal Institute of International Affairs and International Institute for Global Peace, 1993).

60. David Bar-Ilan (director of Communications and Policy Planning in the office of the prime minister), interview with Victor Cygielman, *Palestine-Israel Journal* (summer/autumn 1996). Among Bar-Ilan's other noteworthy observations is that Lebanon "has been able to attack us and make our lives intolerable for more than 15 years," a statement that might not be easy to match in the annals of apologetics for state terrorism.

61. Bill Freund, *The Making of Contemporary Africa* (Bloomington: University of Indiana Press, 1984), 270.

62. Asher Davidi, *Davar,* 17 February 1993; Michael Yudelman, "Labor Government Ready to Take on Labor Unions," *Jerusalem Post,* 26 November 1993; Yaakov Yona, "The Peace Process as an Obstacle to Employment," *Maariv,* 19 January 1996. On the use of transfer threats to undermine labor organizing, accelerating since the NAFTA agreement with Mexico (illegal, but "tolerated by administrations from Reagan through Clinton"), see Cornell University labor economist Kate Bronfenbrenner, "We'll Close," *Multinational Monitor* (March 1997), based on the study she directed, "Final Report: The Effects of Plant Closing or Threat of Plant Closing on the Right of Workers to Organize." The study, conducted under NAFTA rules, in response to labor complaints of violations (upheld after a long delay but with trivial penalties, as is the norm), was authorized for release by Canada and Mexico, but has so far been blocked by Clinton's Labor Department.

63. See Ronen Bergman and David Ratner, "The Man Who Swallowed Gaza," *Ha'aretz Supplement,* 4 April 1997; David Hirst, "Shameless in Gaza," *Guardian Weekly,* 27 April 1997; Judy Dempsey, "Poor Pickings in Gaza for Palestinian Entrepreneurs," *Financial Times,* 3/4 May, reviewing also Israeli economic sabotage; "The Netanyahu Government Will Pay the PLO about ($1.5 Billion) a Year," *Nekuda,* April 1997; David Bedein, "So Much for Promises," *Jerusalem Post,* 4 February 1996.

64. IMF, David Gardner, *Financial Times,* 7 March 1997. UNRWA, Reuters, *New York Times,* May 27, 1997; Peter Kiernan, *Middle East International,* 27 June 1997. Dayan, Herzog, quoted from internal discussions in Beilin, *Mehiro shel Ihud,* 42.147.

65. See Epilogue, *World Orders,* citing *Report on Israeli Settlement,* March 1996; chronology, *Palestine-Israel Journal* (summer/autumn 1996); Nadav Shragai, *Ha'aretz,* 3 March 1997; Beilin quoted by Tikva Honig-Parnass, *News from Within,* April 1997.

66. See Epilogue, *World Orders.*

67. Aluf Ben, *Ha'aretz,* 7 February 1995.

68. Kadoumi, interview, *Frontline* (India), May 30, 1997, at the Non-Aligned Foreign Ministers Conference in New Delhi; El-Abayad (Embassy of Egypt in Washington, DC) letter, *National Interest* (summer 1997).

69. Yossi Melman, "Dunam after Dunam Amounts to a Billion," *Yom Rishon,* 20 April 1997.

70. Avi Shlaim, *Collusion Across the Jordan* (New York: Columbia University Press, 1988), 491, citing Israel state archives.

2

The June 1967 War as a Turning Point in Israel's Strategic Outlook: Amplified Power with Limited Steering Capacity

Yehezkel Dror

ISRAELI STRATEGIC STEERING CAPACITY PRIOR TO THE JUNE 1967 WAR

Before the June 1967 War, Israel faced grave security problems with its very existence at stake in the face of relentless hostility by most of the Arab world. But its strategic situation was relatively simple and the needed security policy and war doctrine were comparatively clear, or so it seemed: with limited territory and very constrained power sources, Israel had to prevent defeat in war at the lowest cost possible, hoping to convince its Arab neighbors through a chain of wars that they would lose, that there was no possibility to liquidate Israel by force and that, therefore, it should be accepted as a permanent entity in the Middle East.

To achieve this goal, Israeli defense forces had to be based on extensive reserve service. Superiority in the air was essential to prevent disruption of reserve mobilization and to reduce civil casualties. Fighting had to be transferred as rapidly as possible into enemy territory and victory achieved quickly, so as to reduce war costs and reach a decision on the battlefield before the big powers had time to intervene. While additional goals were added to the war doctrine, such as protection of freedom of shipping in the Red Sea, the main goal in war was to achieve a clear-cut battlefield victory.[1]

At the same time, a number of often very successful strategic policies were developed and implemented, such as building the

Dimona nuclear reactor, the "peripheral policy" of strategic cooperation with actors surrounding hostile Arab states, and seeking close
relations with at least one major power such as France. But a
broader Clausewitzian view of war as an instrument of statecraft
was beyond the capacities of Israel, and no realistic options of ex-
changing assets gained in war for peace were available.

This picture is oversimplified, ignoring numerous refinements in
Israeli security and military thinking and many divergences between Israeli war plans and unintended consequences.[2] But, all in
all, circumstances provided limited freedom of movement, and the
development of a fitting, rather simple, security strategy was not
very difficult, however exacting may have been its implementation
under given constraints.

In contrast to very good military operational thinking and action,
strategic steering capacities were fragmented and underdeveloped.
Early proposals to set up in the Israeli Defense Forces a Planning
Branch to engage in strategic thinking were not approved, with
some minor and temporary exceptions. Neither the office of the
minister of defense nor the office of the prime minister had any
strategic planning staffs, as distinct from individual advisers. The
pressure of current events, combined with the scarcity of highly
qualified strategic planning professionals on the one hand, and
with cultural features of an "action and ideology driven" political
and governmental culture on the other, created a situation that
tended to prevent high quality strategic thinking. The recognition
that Israeli strategic options were very limited, and, therefore, the
scope for strategic steering very narrow, served as a main additional
reason, however tacit, for lack of efforts to develop a high-quality
strategic steering capacity.

However important these and other causes are in explaining the
weaknesses of Israeli strategic steering capacities before the June
1967 War, it is important to emphasize that existing capacities were
quite adequate for their tasks and, generally, served Israel well.
Even the Sinai campaign fiasco can be explained as a case of reasonable miscalculation rather than a lack of deep strategic thinking.
It may have been a mistake not to learn from this and other failures
that the politico-strategic situation of Israel was more multidimen-
sional than it seemed to be on the surface, and hence, more thinking
on complexities was necessary to prepare for opportunities and
crises. However, this was not the accepted view at that time. Some
important conclusions were drawn from the Sinai campaign, as

well as from other episodes of conflict with Arab neighbors. But Israeli strategic steering remained in the main fragmented, and, in part, primitive, especially after David Ben-Gurion left the scene.

THE JUNE 1967 WAR: OVERLOAD OF INADEQUATE STRATEGIC THINKING

Good strategic thinking could have easily reached the estimation that, in the long run, Israel would become increasingly vulnerable to a determined Arab attack and very hard to defend within its pre-June 1967 War borders once Arab armies underwent modernization. Therefore, good strategic thinking would have concluded that either Israel had to make a determined effort to reach a stable peace settlement, or seek an opportunity to improve its geostrategic situation by breaking out from its 1967 borders.

Israel had no assets that could be exchanged for peace and Arab states at that time showed little inclination to accept Israel as a permanent entity in the Middle East. Therefore, seeking an opportunity to occupy additional territory and then use it to achieve peace together with improved borders should have been Israel's major strategic objective. But, as far as is known, this was not the case. No plans to initiate a war aiming at improving Israel's geostrategic situation were formulated, and, less excusable morally and from the perspective of *Realpolitik*, no plans to use a war initiated by the Arab countries in order to achieve long-term strategic advantages were prepared. Therefore, Israel was completely unprepared for the strategic opportunities provided by the June 1967 War.[3]

It is quite possible that the June 1967 War saved Israel from defeat in a likely later war for which Arab countries would be better prepared. But the history of the June 1967 War and its aftermath clearly shows that Israel lacked strategic steering that might have sought such an opportunity, prepared for it, undertaken it, and then utilized its achievements.

The Israeli victory and achievements in the June 1967 War provided it with strategic security while making it into a major power in the Middle East. These, in turn, laid the geostrategic foundations for Israel's special relationship with the United States, providing a major impetus for its demographic and economic development, and assets essential for peace between Israel and its neighbors. However, these achievements were the results of grave mistakes on the Arab side, combined with Israeli military effectiveness, with luck also playing a role. Thus, the accomplishments emerged despite the lack of Israeli strategic steering, not due to any forethought.

Indeed, lack of adequate strategic steering was a major cause of grievous mistakes, of omission and commission, during the June 1967 War and after it. Thus, during and after the war, Israel could have made a determined effort to try and move toward peace by a partial unilateral withdrawal. Alternatively, Israel could have used the war to transform demographic realities in Judea and Samaria. Instead, a chain of haphazard settlement decisions, not worthy to be called a policy, were made. These decisions resulted in too many Jewish settlements in Judea and Samaria to make withdrawal in a "peace for land" deal easy, and too few settlements to change demographic realities and integrate large parts of the West Bank into Israel.[4]

In short, the June 1967 War overwhelmed Israeli strategic steering. This is an important part of the explanation of the paradox that the war constituted a tremendous Israeli achievement but also resulted in major Israeli failures.

FAILURES OF VICTORY

The June 1967 War put Israel into a radically different situation than before, with a much greater capacity for action and potential for the evolution of different outcomes, but also with many complexities. In order to cope with the new reality while engaging in the intricacies, very high quality strategic planning became a must. Such capacities, however, were not developed. A number of important strategic lessons were drawn from the June 1967 War, some correct and others mistaken. Thus, the doctrine to independently develop some major weapon systems was adopted following the experience of the French embargo. However, no leap in strategic steering capacities equal to the leap in Israeli strategic power took place.

It is interesting to consider the causes for the growing gap between increasing opportunities provided by the achievements of the June 1967 War on the one hand and the lack of proportional improvement of capacities to utilize these opportunities, including the required high-quality strategic steering, on the other. Before the June 1967 War, there was an increase in governmental interest in improving policy thinking. This was a result of a combination of factors, including a feeling of frustration about economic and political difficulties and a growing sense of inadequacy in the face of an historic stalemate exposing Israel to serious dangers. Personal accidents also played a role, with some persons favoring improvements in policy planning reaching very influential positions. International fashions also contributed, with U.S. planning-budgeting-programming systems (PPBS) becoming known to Israeli officials and awakening their interest.

As a result, determined efforts to improve policy planning in the Israeli government were initiated, including an unprecedented six-week residential course for senior officials designated to head "policy planning units." The courses were given with the help of experts from abroad. In addition, there was a formal decision to set up policy planning units in all major ministries; among other initiatives were the preparation of proposals for the prime minister to set up a policy planning staff in his office and initiating an Israeli think tank on the model of the RAND Corporation in the United States.[5]

After the June 1967 War, however, all these efforts ceased; no trace of them remained. The main reason for terminating the efforts to improve policy planning and strategic thinking in Israel was psychological: "If we are so good, as demonstrated by the amazing successes in the June 1967 War, why should we change ourselves"—this was the main line of thinking. It is an irony of history that the very successes of the June 1967 War reinforced the factors hindering efforts to improve strategic steering, with the triumphs viewed as proof that the quality of Israeli strategic decisionmaking was very high and needed no upgrading. The facts, however, were very different. Situations became more complex, new opportunities required a different quality of strategic thinking, the very successes of the June 1967 War were indeed about to produce new problems and dangers—yet, all these were ignored.

This is quite normal for most governments, which seldom learn from mistakes and nearly never from successes. But, still, it is a pity that Israel did not do better. Clearly, its responses to the challenges posed by the achievements of the June 1967 War were inadequate, with failures sure to follow. It took the shock of the Day of Atonement War (1973) for Israel to draw some of the correct conclusions, but adequate strategic steering capacities were still beyond the purview of Israeli policymakers.

Following the failures of the Day of Atonement War, a Planning Branch was set up in the Israeli General Staff, which also serves the minister of defense and the prime minister from time to time. Thus, this unit fulfills major tasks in Israeli planning on the Peace Process. But, essential components of high-quality strategic steering are still missing: integration among military, political, socioeconomic and other dimensions is inadequate; perceptive long-term thinking as a basis for current critical decisions is underdeveloped; and well-trained strategic planning professionals are very scarce, since neither the universities nor the government provide suitable teaching and training for such professionals.

With time, factors inhibiting good strategic steering have become stronger rather than weaker. The ideological aspects of Israeli policies within the peace process inhibit what is termed "cold" strategic steering. Furthermore, daily pressures and crises, such as escalating terrorism, preoccupy the attention of decision makers and staffs alike. Lately, the growing populism driven by the mass media and recent changes in the Israeli political system, especially the introduction of primaries in the major parties, in combination with heated political competition, push toward short-term "blowing of bubbles" rather than long-term thinking. Hopes that direct election of the prime minister would assure adequate strategic-steering frameworks have not yet been fulfilled.

Whatever one's view on the relative weight of these and other factors in explaining the absence of strategic-steering capacities in Israel—capacities that should be equal to the opportunities and dangers posed by the outcomes of the June 1967 War and the many developments since then—there is no doubt that this absence is pronounced. The nonprediction and mishandling of the Intifada, decisions related to the situation in South Lebanon, and some aspects of Israeli choices in relation to the peace process are but a few of the many important illustrations of the results, *inter alia,* of Israeli strategic-steering weaknesses.

CHALLENGE AND RESPONSE

The June 1967 War made Israel into a major regional power, very greatly increasing its capacities to act in the region and opening very many policy options. The disintegration of the Soviet Empire and all that followed further multiplied the power assets of Israel while transforming the situation in the Middle East as a whole. Thanks to some outstanding decision makers in the government, together with some high-quality fragments of strategic thinking, Israel responded well to some of the opportunities. However, all in all, I evaluate Israel's responses to the challenges produced by the June 1967 War metamorphosis as inadequate, irrespective of ideological preferences, which have been democratically presented and decided.

The inadequacy of Israeli policies is only in part a result of lack of high-quality strategic steering. Thus, as in all democracies,[6] coalition constraints limit the options of Israeli decision makers, as do difficulties with consensus building and shifts in public opinion. But better strategic steering could have a significant impact on policies and choices, and its absence surely causes many mistakes and failures that could be avoided despite political and other constraints.

In short, the Six-Day War was a turning point in Israel's strategic situation, but was not accompanied by a proportional turning point in Israel's strategic-steering capacities. This fact is a major cause, though not the only one, of the inadequacy of Israeli responses to the new challenges posed by the June 1967 War and the developments that followed.

Such a cause of failure is relatively easy to overcome, at least in part. It thus stands in contrast to the unavoidable shallowness of public opinion in a democracy. None of the factors hindering better strategic steering poses insurmountable difficulties to leaders and decision makers determined to get better strategic advice, or to professional units determined to provide better strategic advice. Therefore, I tend to the view that one of the really critical causes of the continuing weaknesses in Israeli strategic steering is persistent lack of recognition by high-level decision makers of the crucial importance of improving such capacities. This is a "subjective" cause not dictated by stubborn "objective" realities. Its perseverance carries high costs for Israel that are avoidable and, therefore, in the expected judgment of history, inexcusable.[7]

NOTES

1. The subject is well discussed in Avi Kober, *Military Decision in the Arab-Israeli Wars 1948–1982* (in Hebrew) (Tel Aviv: Maarachot, 1995).

2. For a succinct discussion, see Michael I. Handel, "The Evolution of Israeli Strategy: The Psychology of Insecurity and the Quest for Absolute Security," in *The Making of Strategy: Rulers, States, and War*, edited by Williamson Murray, MacGregor Know, and Alvin Bernstein (Cambridge: Cambridge University Press, 1994), 534–78.

3. Compare Uri Millstein, "The Six Day War: Why Is Israel Abandoning Its Gains?" (in Hebrew), *Nativ* 10, no. 4 (July 1997): 73–77.

4. For an extensively documented study, see Reuven Pedatzur, *The Triumph of Embarrassment: Israel and the Territories after the Six-Day War* (in Hebrew) (Tel Aviv: Bitan, 1996).

5. This information is based on the personal knowledge of the author, who served as chief consultant to the government on the introduction of policy planning.

6. Richard Rosencrance and Arthur A. Stein, eds., *The Domestic Basis of Grand Strategy* (Ithaca, NY: Cornell University Press, 1993).

7. For more detailed discussion of the subjects of this essay, see Yehezkel Dror, *A Grand Strategy for Israel* (in Hebrew) (Jerusalem: Academon, 1989); *Grand Strategic Thinking for Israel*, Policy paper 23 (Ariel, Israel: Ariel Center for Policy Research, 1998).

3

Defeat and Victory: Thirty Years Since the June 1967 War

Musa Budairi

The war that broke out in June 1967 is a pivotal landmark in the contemporary history of the Arab peoples: it threw the Arab world off balance. In its immediate aftermath it led to questioning and self-doubt; the book *Auto Critique in the Aftermath of the Defeat* by Sadek Al Azm, a young radical Syrian philosopher became a bestseller overnight.[1] In retrospect however, it is possible to see that since the demise of the Arab nationalist project, symbolized by Gamal Abdel Nasser and Egypt's leadership of the Arab world and the nonaligned bloc of African and Asian nations, nothing has taken its place.

On June 9, 1967, Nasser delivered a televised address in which he assumed full political responsibility for the devastating military defeat and submitted his resignation. Nasser's resignation brought hundreds of thousands of people into the streets, who seemed to feel instinctively that this act in itself was a consecration of the defeat and a submission to the defeat. They rejected his resignation in a somewhat mystical belief that in acquiescing, they would be according legitimacy to the defeat.

Subsequently, the energies of the Arab states would direct themselves to "liquidating the effects of the aggression," that is, trying to secure Israel's withdrawal from the territories occupied in the war, and bringing about an undefined "just resolution of the refugee problem."[2] For the Arab ruling elites, the struggle with Israel has always been a sideshow, and moreover, one whose pace and intensity was set by Israel.

On the popular level, the future seemed to hold unbound possibilities. The Palestinians assumed center stage, perhaps for the first
time since the defeat of the military uprising unleashed against the
British in 1936–39. Taking advantage of the weakness and loss of legitimacy of the Arab regimes, they launched themselves into the
fight in order to galvanize a dormant Arab world, but one with un-
limited potential. Perhaps along the way, the leadership of the
Palestinian movement wished to emulate the Vietnamese and create another Hanoi that would serve as the base for a military campaign to wage a protracted peoples' war. The Palestinian Resistance
Movement, as it was called at the time, symbolized the spirit of the
times. Thousands of Arab and non-Arab youths joined its ranks. It
appeared to hold the promise of social and political liberation and
empowerment. The Egyptian popular singer Shikh Immam was eu-
logizing Che Guevara and spreading his last testament, addressed,
in his words, "to those chained both mind and feet. . . . [T]o prepare
the army of final salvation, or suffer continuing enslavement."[3]

There were many way stations on the road from the Palestine National Council's adoption of the Transitional program in 1974, spec-
ifying the aim of "a national authority,"[4] to Madrid and Oslo.
Throughout, a triumphalist discourse served to mask a series of de-
feats and retreats that gradually transformed the nature and aims of
the conflict. One salient feature of the conflict, which has remained
constant throughout, has been the Israeli determination and ability
to dictate the terms of the conflict in both peace and war. As early as
1922, Arthur Rupin, an instrumental figure in the history of Jewish
settlement in Palestine, wrote that "on every site where we purchase land and where we settle people, the present cultivators will
inevitably be dispossessed." He arrived at the conclusion a few
years later that "it is our destiny to be in a state of continual warfare with the Arab[s]."[5]

In the absence of a Palestinian adversary in the period up to 1967,
Israel waged a struggle against Egypt and Syria. The major landmarks were the wars launched in 1956 and 1967, but there was also a
continuous and persistent war going on all the time. A war directed
not against armies and states, but against ordinary people in Egypt,
Syria, Jordan, Lebanon, and further afield. The aim was to ground the
Arabs, both individually and collectively, into submission.

Israel has a long record of visiting death and destruction at will:
Qibya, Galza, Al Samou', Bahr al Bakar, Irbid, Beirut, Hammam Al
Shat, Qana, are names of some of the major places where Israel in-

flicted death and suffering upon Arabs.[6] More recently, southern Lebanon was submitted to a massive bombardment, and nearly half a million people were given eight hours notice to leave their homes, whereupon their villages were transformed into military targets, and sixteen thousand shells were rained on them.

Let me repeat. Whether as an adjunct to its nation-building project, or as an ideological imperative in fulfillment of a messianic vision, the policies pursued by Israel have visited death and destruction on the surrounding Arab populations. Such acts are perhaps grounded in the belief that it is not enough to possess the military capability to inflict strategic punishment on the surrounding states and hold them in a state of perpetual military inferiority, but that it is necessary to achieve the surrender of Arabs individually as well as collectively, and cow them into submission. Indeed, attacks on the Arab populations of neighboring states was standard Israeli practice long before the Begins, Sharons, Shamirs, and Netanyahus made their debut on the political stage as legitimate representatives of the Israeli body politic.

As Arye Shavit wrote (ironically) in *Haaretz* after the massacre at Qana in Lebanon in 1996, "with Dimona, Yad Vashem and the Shoa Museum in Israel, this gives the country the right to kill without entertaining any guilt feelings."[7] The situation has not changed in the aftermath of Madrid and Oslo; Fathi Shakkaki in Malta, Yehia Ayyash in Gaza, one hundred and two people in Qana, and, most recently, Khaled Abu Dayeh in the emergency room at Shaarei Tzedek Hospital in Jerusalem, were killed by Israelis.[8] The botched assassination attempt of Khaled Mishaal in Jordan confirms that state terrorism is still Israel's weapon of choice.[9] Both individually and collectively, the killing goes on, and the Israeli legal system itself lends a hand, sanctioning torture to extract confessions from Palestinian suspects under what is euphemistically termed "moderate physical pressure." Israeli newspapers reveal that such torture includes "shaking," from which a few Palestinians have perished.

To an overwhelming degree, Israel has succeeded in implementing its political and military agenda in the region. Transjordan under Abdullah was neutralized in the prestate period, while Jordan under Hussein has proven to be Israel's neighbor of choice. We are currently approaching what promises to be the final cycle of the Arab-Israeli conflict, ushered in by the conclusion of a separate peace at Camp David that served to detach Egypt from the leadership of the Arab world and paved the way for the 1982 invasion of

Lebanon and the occupation of the first Arab capital. Israel's so far successful decision to enroll the Palestinians in its efforts to ensure a hegemonic presence in the Arab world by having the Palestinians acquiesce to an offer of limited self-rule, has created further divisions and allowed some members of a hesitant Arab world to normalize relations at the state level. Significantly, a columnist in a leading Arab newspaper that is today a steadfast champion of the peace process, asked on the anniversary of Nasser's death two years ago, whether the time had not come to "bury Nasser," as this was a necessary act if the Arabs were to qualify to enter the ranks of the community of "civilised nations!"[10]

The cumulative effect of these policies has been a contributing factor to the ongoing Palestinian weakness in the "peace process." Furthermore, the failure of the Palestinians to enlist the Arab world on their behalf has resulted in their conversion to the belief that the only viable option open to them is to arrive at an arrangement that fits in with Israel's own strategic requirements. This is neither the long-heralded historic compromise, nor the much touted "peace of the brave."

The PLO that has been recognized by Israel, and whose leadership has been allowed to set up camp in strictly designated areas of the still Occupied Territories (which brings to mind the phrase of Rafael Eitan, chief of staff at the time of the 1982 Israeli invasion of Lebanon, who said that Israel should relate to the Palestinians as if they were cockroaches in a bottle),[11] is a PLO with a new agenda. Having severed itself from the main body of the Palestinian people, who remain unable to return to the land of Palestine, it has agreed to abandon the demand for the dismantling of settlements, and has to all intents and purposes submitted to a new partition within the 23 percent of the territory of mandated Palestine, which was occupied in June 1967. Perhaps, more significantly, it finds it hard to shrug off the task it has been entrusted with as a condition for this arrangement, namely to carry out the role of guardian of Israel's security.

In the prevailing culture of defeat and submission, the voices of those refusing to succumb seem discordant and irrational, perhaps even psychotic. The response of many Palestinian people to the 1991 Gulf War, irrespective of the rights and wrongs of the occupation of Kuwait and the nature of the Iraqi regime, was a manifestation of a deep-seated yearning to be able to stand up and hit back. This was encapsulated by a statement made by a random Palestin-

ian interviewee during the scud attacks on Israel, in response to ac-
cusations that Palestinians were in favor of Saddam and his Kuwaiti
adventure. The interviewee stated that the favorable Palestinian response to the attack on Israel had nothing to do with Iraq, Kuwait,
or the wish to annihilate Israel, and everything to do with the fact
that for the first time the missiles were going the other way.

Israel continues to be at one and the same time triumphalist and
paranoid. It craves recognition. It demands that the victims of its
very act of creation stand up and proclaim the justness of its cause.
The persistence of the Palestinian claim, even if merely rhetorical, or
captured in a line of verse by Mahmoud Darweesh,[12] in and of itself
poses a threat that conjures up fear and insecurity. In the service of
this "security discourse," all manners of oppression of Palestinians
by Israel are justified.

The claim is often made that one cannot lay the blame on the Israeli political and military elite for their inability to convince the Israeli masses of the necessity of arriving at a just settlement. We
Palestinians are told that it is the inhabitants of towns like Dimona
and Beit Shemesh who set the political agenda in a democratic society such as Israel. But the political diet that is presented to them
is not of their own making. Most recently, we had the revelations of
Moshe Dayan's interview in the 1970s, in which he spoke about the
situation at the settlements neighboring the Golan Heights in the
pre-1967 period and the "manufacture" of violent incidents in order
to annex demilitarized areas to Israel.[13] In that interview, Dayan also
mentioned the absence of any security threat from the Syrians after
the outbreak of war with Egypt. For years, Israelis and the world
were fed the story of a belligerent Syria that was continuously violating armistice agreements and bombarding Israeli settlements.

More recently, a former chief of Israeli intelligence appeared on
an Arab owned TV station on the eve of the anniversary of June 5,
1967 and explained that Israel finds itself in a difficult situation because it can only make peace with democratic states, and none of its
neighbors qualify. This seemed a rather strange statement to make
considering Israel's favored Arab regimes are the hereditary monarchies of Morocco and Jordan, and that prerevolutionary Iran and
apartheid South Africa were among its closest allies. For those of us
who remember the hysteria generated on the eve of the war, the expected annihilation, and then the miracle that unfolded and led to
the speedy capture of territories in Egypt, Syria, and Jordan, the recent revelations of another former senior intelligence official about

his trip to the United States on the eve of the June 1967 War and his talks with Secretary McNamara,[14] seem to confirm all the conspiracy theories that were brought forward at the time: that this was a war with American blessing aimed at destroying Nasser's regime. The forecasts of the length of hostilities and the expected casualties show what kind of stuff miracles are made of! They also uncover that the manipulation of public opinion by Israeli leaders was not only aimed at journalists and people abroad, but more importantly at the Israeli people themselves.

Despite such revelations, which of course can only possess validity when they are expressed by Israeli officials or former officials, Israel continues to exhibit a wounded innocence and to profess total ignorance of the Other. Initially, the claim was that ignorance prevailed among Israelis because it was impossible for the newcomers to know that this was an inhabited land; they were after all children of their own time, and imbued with the biases and prejudices common to other Europeans. On arrival, they discovered the Arab inhabitants for the first time, but of course as Europeans they tended to discount them as merely *natives*. The sad narrative of bad faith continues: those who came after 1948 and those who were born here thereafter could not have possibly known that others were living here previously. The 160,000 or so Arabs who succeeded in remaining within the borders of the Jewish state led a secluded life, shrouded from sight until at least 1966 by the workings of the military government. In the aftermath of 1967, Arabs were discovered living in the West Bank and Gaza. This was a revelation. It was "the first time" Israelis came face-to-face with a full-fledged Arab society. In 1982, after the invasion of Lebanon, the three-month-long siege, the massacres at Sabra and Shattila, and the conquest of Beirut, the Israelis again "for the first time" came face-to-face with the demonized enemy. Again, this was the "first meeting" with the Palestinians. In 1987, the Intifada broke out in the territories that had been under Israeli control for more than twenty years, and again for "the first time" the Israelis discovered Palestinians; they also discovered that the occupation was not and indeed could not be enlightened. But then, of course, such is the nature of occupations, and all knowledgeable Israelis professed that they knew that!

For many Palestinians, it is not clear if what Israelis suffer from is blindness or self-delusion. One thing, however, is clear, and that is that they do not see themselves as part of this neighborhood, this area of the world. Indeed, they do not like this neighborhood but for some reason (which they almost never question), they find themselves living in it, and they have to be permanently on guard. The Palestinians who live in close proximity, within this neighborhood, and who keep being discovered for "the first time," and their own relationship to the neighborhood are neither part of the everyday perceptions and thoughts of many Israelis, nor of their world vision. This myopia is not the affliction of traditionalists or those coming from Arab backgrounds; it is a widespread disease. Those Israelis who have been blessed with the ability of partial vision have achieved this state of grace as a result of their exposure to the work of revisionist writers, who after painstaking research of the words and acts of the founding fathers of Israel and various state officials, have raised questions regarding the veracity of accepted wisdom. As one Israeli put it sadly:

But of course all this happened long ago. . . . It happened in many other places in similar circumstances. . . . It is part and parcel of the process of nation building and state formation. The [Palestinian] people of Yalu and Emmwas and Beit Nuba [whom Israelis forcefully evacuated from their homes and then destroyed their villages] wherever they are today, know and remember what happened in 1967. But for [Israeli] picnickers in Canada Park [which was established on the ruins of these villages] we are already living in the Post Oslo period.[15]

This is what victory and defeat are all about.

NOTES

1. Sadek Al-Azm, *Auto Critique in the Aftermath of the Defeat* (Beirut, 1968).

2. At the Khartoum Arab Summit held in August 1967, Arab leaders adopted the famous three No's: No Peace with Israel, No recognition of Israel, No negotiations with Israel. See Charles D. Smith, *Palestine and the Arab Israeli Conflict* (New York, 1988), 210–11.

3. A. F. Nejem, *Baladi Wa Habibati* (Beirut, 1973), 5.

4. The twelfth Palestine National Council was held in Cairo on June 1, 1974, and adopted the Ten Point Programme, which for the first time spoke of a Palestinian National Authority. See A. Gresh, *The PLO, The Struggle Within: Towards an Independent Palestinian State* (London, 1985), 167–71.

5. See A. Gorny, *Zionism and the Arabs 1882–1948, A Study in Ideology* (Oxford, 1987), 246.

6. For the earlier period see Benny Morris, *Israel's Border Wars 1949–1956* (Oxford, 1993).

7. Arye Shavit, "Qana: 102 Faceless Dead" (in Hebrew), *Haaretz*, 3 April 1997.

8. Gideon Levy, "Manslaughter in Shaarei Zedek" (in Hebrew), *Haaretz*, 1 June 1997.

9. *Haaretz*, 5 October 1997.

10. Abdul Wahab Badrakhan writing in the London based *Al-Hayat*, September 1994.

11. Raphael Eitan is currently head of Tzomet party, and a cabinet minister in Netanyahu's government.

12. Mahmoud Darweesh is a Palestinian poet who at the time was a member of the executive committee of the PLO. His 1988 poem, "Those Who Pass Between Fleeting Words," is in Z. Lockman and J. Beinin, eds., *Intifada: The Palestinian Uprising against Israeli Occupation* (Boston: South End Press, 1989), 26–27.

13. Rami Tal, "Interviews with Moshe Dayan on November 1976 and January 1977" (in Hebrew), *Yediot Ahronot*, 27 April 1997.

14. "Interview with Meir Amit," *Haaretz*, 13 May 1997.

15. The extract mentions three villages in the Latrun area that were destroyed and their inhabitants evicted in the immediate aftermath of the June 1967 War. The Israeli writer, Amos Kenan, who witnessed the expulsion of the inhabitants while serving in the army, wrote an account of the incident. See G. Aronson, *Creating Facts: Israel, Palestinians and the West Bank* (Washington, DC: 1987), 19.

Part II

Israeli-Palestinian Relations

4

A Lost Opportunity: A Buberian Outlook on the Occupation

Haim Gordon

Martin Buber passed away in Jerusalem in 1965, two years before the June 1967 War. This war, and the thirty years that followed, brought great changes in the Middle East, in Israel, and among the Palestinians. Some of the changes will be described and evaluated at this conference. Despite his wisdom, it is dubious that Buber could have foreseen many of the details of these changes. Yet, we can ask if we Israelis, especially we Jewish Israelis, attempted to realize during these years some of the principles that Martin Buber believed in and taught. The immediate answer is that aside from a very small struggling minority of us, Buber's thoughts have been very much ignored. Very few struggled to realize them. I can say categorically, that as a nation: No. We Israelis did not at all attempt to learn from Buber's thinking how to relate to the opportunity that was opened in the wake of the June 1967 War. I fear that many Jews in Israel still firmly reject this opportunity. What is this opportunity? In what ways are we rejecting it? How has this rejection influenced our daily existence? These are questions that I will briefly attempt to answer.

It would be not too great a challenge to partially explain this lost opportunity on the basis of Buber's political views. Over almost half a century, in many short political statements and in articles and speeches, Buber emphasized the need for dialogue and genuine sharing with the Arabs living in Palestine and in other countries of the Middle East. He repeatedly demanded that Jews live justly with their Arab neighbors, and respect the rights of the Arabs who live in Palestine. Paul Mendes-Flohr has done a great service to Buber scholarship and Zionist history and thinking in publishing a book in which Buber's writings in this area are collected.[1] Here, however, I wish to begin by explaining this lost opportunity from the perspective of Buber's ontology and theology. It will soon be evident that this ontology and theology lead to specific political views. There is much more justice to such an approach, I believe, since Buber's major contributions to contemporary thought were in the fields of philosophy and theology.

It is broadly accepted that Buber's main contribution to philosophy and theology is his book, *I and Thou*. The opening sentence of the book states: "To man the world is twofold, in accordance with his twofold attitude."[2] Buber explains that this twofold world and attitude are concentrated in two primary or basic words: I-Thou and I-It. A major difference between these attitudes is that the Thou is uttered with one's whole being, in a moment of being truly present to the Other, while the It is never uttered with one's whole being. The Other, for Buber, is what concretely confronts me, be it a natural being, such as this willow tree, a person, or a spiritual being, for instance, a symphony by Beethoven. Buber's descriptions of the many important distinctions between the I-Thou and the I-It are lucid, while often bordering on the poetic. Yet, one distinction repeatedly emerges, even if Buber did not always formulate it in the manner that I will now formulate it. It is the distinction between sharing and manipulating. The I-Thou is basically an attitude of sharing with the Other, in which you relate dialogically to the person or the being confronting you. The I-It is basically an attitude of manipulating the Other.

Buber stated quite clearly that he is not creating an unneeded dichotomy between the I-Thou and the I-It. His book, *I and Thou*, is first and foremost a phenomenological description of human reality. It is not an ethical treatise. Yet, this book is also a resounding call to each reader to make space for the I-Thou attitude in one's life and in the world. It is a call to us readers to relate dialogically. Buber recognizes that one cannot live more than a short period of time fully in the presence that is crucial for the I-Thou attitude. He clearly states: "But this is the exalted melancholy of our fate, that every Thou in our world must become an It."[3] Yet Buber also holds that a person who lives solely in the I-It attitude, and never or hardly ever relates as a Thou, such a person has abandoned a crucial aspect of one's humanity.

Buber recognizes that there is a risk involved in endeavoring to adopt the I-Thou attitude in as many instances as possible, including in the political realm. Yet, he also stresses that opening oneself to the possibility of relating to the Other as a Thou can create marvelous opportunities. Love is one of these opportunities; sharing and friendship are additional opportunities. Living responsibly, by striving to share justly with others, is another opportunity—this opportunity arises in the political realm and has many political implications. These opportunities disappear when a person's being is governed by the I-It attitude, when a person directs one's being solely to manipulating the Other.

Even with this very brief description of Buber's ontology, we Jewish Israelis can look back at thirty years since the June 1967 War and ask two simple questions: What has been the basic attitude that we have adopted toward the Palestinian population that Israel has ruled since 1967? Did this attitude change over the years? The answers are evident. For thirty years the large majority of Israelis have adopted an I-It attitude toward the Palestinians. Furthermore, for thirty years, the governments of Israel have related to the Palestinians in the Occupied Territories as Its, as human beings that exist solely to be manipulated for Israel's needs and interests. Despite the signing of the peace accords, my impression is that, unfortunately, little has changed in this basic attitude toward the Palestinians, neither at the level of government decisions, nor at the level of personal interaction.

Can a person strive to relate to the Other with whom one has deep political disagreements as a Thou? Buber answered a definite: Yes. I want to lend support to Buber's view by mentioning three great political leaders of the twentieth century whose biographies reveal them as responsibly struggling for the freedom of their people, while striving to relate to their political antagonists as Thous. They are Mahatma Mohandas Gandhi, Jawaharlal Nehru, and Nelson Mandela. In accordance with Buber's approach, I wish to add that, at least according to their writings, Gandhi and Nehru were also spiritual leaders, who believed that the political realm is a realm in which leaders and lay people should pursue justice daily. The same is true of Nelson Mandela who is still striving for justice in his country and in the world. Their deeds often accord with Buber's writing on the political leader in *I and Thou*:

The statesman or the economist who obeys the spirit is no dilettante; he knows well that he cannot, without undoing his work, simply confront, as bearers of the *Thou*, the men with whom he has to deal. Yet he risks doing it, not plainly and simply, but as far as the boundary set for him by the spirit.[4]

We can now partially begin to perceive some elements of the lost opportunity of these past thirty years. A major element is the lost opportunity of pursuing justice with our neighbors, the Palestinians. We Israelis deliberately lost the opportunity to live responsibly in the spirit of dialogue with them. Instead of seeking justice and sharing, we oppressed and exploited the Palestinians daily, manipulating them as Its, refusing to relate to them as Thous. This situation still exists. Consider the Gaza Strip: 90 percent of the population, 900,000 people, are forced to live confined from the world, behind a guarded fence, because they can never receive Israeli permission to leave the area, or because they are so steeped in poverty, that even if they received permission, they could not find the means to travel. Israel has converted the Gaza Strip into a ghetto sixty kilometers long and fourteen kilometers wide at its broadest points. Forcing people to live in a ghetto by economic and political means is an example of Israeli oppression, of Israel's manipulation of hundreds of thousands of Palestinians. Think of it, today, four years after the peace accords, fifty kilometers from here, 900,000 people are locked behind a fence in an area that they can never leave.

Buber very clearly held that a person who forgoes his or her opportunity to relate to the Other as a Thou and to pursue justice is ruining one's soul. I would hold, as a student of Buber, that a nation made up of a large majority of people who refuse to relate to our Palestinian neighbors as Thous is a nation of ruined souls. The superficiality and hollowness that characterizes much of Israeli political and spiritual life in these past thirty years suggests that there is much truth in Buber's statement. One of the most prominent examples of this superficiality and hollowness, an example that is again firmly linked to Buber's thinking, is Jewish religious existence, to which I now turn.

I believe that Buber would have noted that one of the saddest developments in religious life among Jews in Israel in the past thirty years is the spread of idol worshiping. What is unique about this idolatry is that much of it is dictated by nationalist political views and comes from Jews who call themselves religious. Indeed, from a sociotheological perspective, we are confronted with a very revolting, yet interesting phenomenon, whereby idol worshiping in many so-called religious circles has become the norm, and from these circles it is spreading, like a cancer, to nonreligious Jews. What is no less repulsive is that from among the so-called religious Jews, not one major rabbi or political leader has come forward to condemn this idolatry.

Let me concentrate briefly on one example of this idolatry. Nowhere in the Bible, as far as I know, is it mentioned that the city of Hebron is holy. In his book, *On Zion,* Buber briefly indicates that the development of the concept of a holy land developed in Jewish thought quite late, at the earliest in the Talmudic period. In the Bible, the land of Canaan is promised to Abraham so that his progeny may serve God here in true faith. The land is promised, but the promise does not insure that Israel will live on the land, nor does it make the land as such holy, since for centuries before Israel came to the land, it was populated by idol worshipers. Moreover, the Hebrew prophets repeatedly stated that once the progeny of Abraham abandon the true faith, which includes living in justice, the land will vomit them out.

During the Biblical period, no hill, or mountain, or grove of trees, or city is designated holy. In his book, *The Prophetic Faith,* Buber explains that the Bible describes holy events, but not holy persons or places. A holy event occurs only when the spirit of God is present. A place, such as the tent of the holy ark, may become holy for a period of time if the spirit of God rests there. But this holy ark has no powers when it is used by Israel merely as a means to gain a military victory, as described in the book of Samuel I. A person can be invaded by the *ruach,* the spirit of God, as the prophets were invaded by the Godly spirit. But this invasion does not make these persons holy. When the Hebrew prophets speak the words of God, they can help establish a holy event, as Elijah did on the peak of Mount Carmel when he challenged the prophets of the Baal. But neither Elijah nor Mount Carmel became holy as a result of this holy event. Consequently, today, for a Jew or a group of Jews to designate a place or a city as holy, has no basis in the Bible. Such a designating is idolatry.

Since the June 1967 War, hundreds of fanatical rabbis and their quite ignorant followers have decided that many areas in the Occupied Territories are holy, including the city of Hebron. These decisions have allowed them to act in ways that totally reject the Decalogue. Thus, the followers of these rabbis, notable among them are Levinger and Kahane, but they are not alone, have murdered Palestinians and stolen their property, thus breaking the commandments Thou shall not murder and Thou shall not steal. In addition, these followers of fanatical rabbis have sworn false testimony against the Palestinians and coveted the land and property of the Palestinians, thus breaking the commandments Thou shall not bear false witness against thy neighbor and Thou shall not covet thy neighbor's house . . . nor anything that is thy neighbor's. Perhaps the most ugly sin of some of these rabbis is that they have glorified Baruch Goldstein, the mass murderer of twenty-nine unarmed Moslems who were praying in what is called Abraham's tomb.

Consequently, with full sanction and staunch support from hundreds of rabbis in Israel, thousands of Jews, many among them settlers, have acted in stark contradiction to four of the last five commandments. Note that these Jewish sinners and criminals, including Baruch Goldstein, have broken these commandments in the name of the so-called holiness of the city of Hebron and other so-called holy places. In short, these sinning rabbis, and especially the rabbis in the settlements in the Occupied Territories and their followers, have not only ignored the dialogical aspect of the Bible that Buber wrote about. They have also daily broken Judaism's most basic law, the Ten Commandments, which centuries of Jewish leaders and thinkers, among them Martin Buber, held in high esteem.

Through their actions these hundreds of rabbis, who are often supported by the silence of many hundreds of other rabbis in Israel and the world, have taught that the Ten Commandments are not what is important in Judaism. What is important, they wrongly teach, is the areas of land that they have designated as holy. Thus, since the June 1967 War, rabbis, politicians, and religious parties in Israel have promoted an interpretation of Judaism that includes a firm rejection of the commandments given by God to Moses on Mount Sinai, at the most important event in the history of Israel. This evil and sacrilegious approach is promoted by leading rabbis, including past and present chief rabbis. Unfortunately, these evil religious leaders are called by their followers the spiritual teachers of Judaism.

Let me therefore say at once. These rabbis are not spiritual leaders. They are fakes. They resemble the false prophets whom Elijah put to test and finally killed on Mount Carmel. They are not followers of Elijah or of the other Hebrew prophets. For two simple reasons. First, justice never concerns them, and second, they worship sites in the land as the prophets of the Baal did. This statement deserves repeating. Hundreds of rabbis in Israel today are idol worshipers because instead of a commitment to living in justice, in accordance with the Decalogue, they encourage their followers to reject commandments and to worship instead sites in the land of Israel. This attitude is precisely the idol worship that the Hebrew prophets continually denounced and against which they firmly, and at times fiercely, struggled. Need I add that Martin Buber repeatedly rejected such idol worship in his writings?

Were he living today, it is probable that Martin Buber might have also concluded that since this idolatry has become central to the consciousness of many Jews in the past thirty years, it is no surprise that a leading rabbi, Ovadiah Yosef, sanctioned the selling of charms and amulets in the last elections so as to gain political power. These are actions, every student of Buber would probably add, that Jeremiah, Isaiah, Amos, and other prophets would have firmly condemned. Yet today, Ovadiah Yosef, who daily spreads idolatry in Judaism, is considered to be one of Judaism's most authentic and prominent spokesmen. Buber strictly rejected all such idolatry, including adulation of persons, such as the unwarranted adulation that surrounds Ovadiah Yosef. Learning from Buber, I believe that when Judaism's leaders commit themselves to the sin of idolatry, by worshiping sites in the land and teaching their followers that it is correct to break God's Ten Commandments, the idolatry spreads to all areas of life, including the selling of charms and amulets in the political realm.

Someone might intervene and ask: Aren't you exaggerating in your attacks against the rabbis in the settlements and their ardent supporters? After all, some of the rabbis who reside in the settlements declare that they support peace and dialogue with the Palestinians. Why do you denounce all these rabbis?

Let me give one example of a rabbi who is considered to be at the extreme left of the rabbis who reside in the settlements in the Occupied Territories, and who has been almost ostracized by his fellow rabbis and settlers for his so-called leftist views, Rabbi Yoel Bin Noon. After the assassination of Yitzhak Rabin, it was Yoel Bin Noon who called upon his fellow religious leaders and fellow members of the National Religious Party to acknowledge their blame in creating the atmosphere that led to the murder of the prime minister. Bin Noon was vehemently attacked by many rabbis, party members, and settlers for these statements. He even received threatening phone calls. What, therefore, are Bin Noon's views concerning fulfilling the Ten Commandments, dialogue with the Palestinians, and sharing this land with them?

Bin Noon presented his views in an essay in the May 1994 issue of *Nekuda,* the monthly publication of the settlers.[5] In that essay, he points out that there is no possibility of continuing to oppress the Palestinians since most of the Jews in Israel are against this oppression. He acknowledges that Israel will have to give land to the Palestinians, despite what he calls our historical right. He mentions no such rights for the Palestinians. He proposes what he calls a pragmatic approach. Israel should immediately confiscate, annex, and settle large tracts of land in the Occupied Territories. The rest of the land will be given up. He adds that any Jew who leaves a settlement on the West Bank or in the Gaza Strip is a deserter. Since May 1994, Bin Noon has frequently written in other periodicals and newspapers, elaborating his so-called pragmatic approach.

In simple words, Rabbi Yoel Bin Noon, the supposed leftist rabbi of the settlers, is coveting the homes and land of the Palestinians and suggesting that we rob them of their land. He is thus suggesting that we break two of the Ten Commandments. No, suggesting is too mild a word. Rabbi Bin Noon is inciting his readers and students to break two of the Ten Commandments in the name of his idolatry of the land of Israel. Nowhere in his writings has Bin Noon ever suggested relation dialogically to the Palestinians, or considering them to be Thous with whom we share this area as sojourners on Earth. For Bin Noon, the Palestinians are Its, they are to be manipulated to serve Jewish interests. Note, in passing, that the word pragmatic never appears in the Bible. I suspect that the Hebrew prophets, who demanded that we pursue justice and genuine faith in God, never needed such a word. Evidently, the idol worshiper, Rabbi Yoel Bin Noon, needs such a word.

Thus, as a student of Buber I must sadly state: In the past thirty years we Jews have lost the opportunity to live a worthy and authentic religious life based on the demand for justice and the dialogical teaching of the prophets, and in accordance with the Decalogue. After the June 1967 War, instead of opening a dialogue with the Palestinians, we relegated them to the role of a captive people, subject to our whims, our greed, and our will to power. Instead of acknowledging the Palestinians as neighbors, as people living on the land to which both peoples have strong historical ties, as part-

ners in this area of the world, we Jews brutally oppressed and cru-
elly exploited them. We learned little from the spiritual message of
Buber and the Hebrew prophets that a religious life is lived in the
everyday deed done in the spirit of dialogue, and with great responsibility for justice in every moment of decision.

Our so-called religious leaders are greatly to blame for this lost
opportunity. They justified our evil deeds by developing astute Talmudic justifications, not only for rejecting dialogue with the Palestinians, but also for killing them, robbing them, bearing false
testimony against them, and coveting their property. Judaism, as
promoted by these rabbis, has lost the opportunity of living in justice and true faith, in the spirit of Moses, Isaiah, Jeremiah, and our
other prophets. Judaism, as promoted by Ovadiah Yosef and hundreds of other rabbis, has become a fanatical inane religion, lacking
the spirituality of the Bible. It is rabbis such as these that Isaiah condemned in chapter 1 verse 21:

> How is the faithful city become a harlot
> She that was full of justice, righteousness lodged in her,
> but now murderers.

Many secular Jews are also to blame for the lost opportunity of
living justly in the spirit of dialogue with the Palestinians and with
our other Arab neighbors. Among the settlers on land confiscated
from Palestinians live thousands of secular Jews. Furthermore,
only a small minority of Jews in Israel rejected the constant oppression and exploitation of Palestinians during the two decades
before the Intifada. Indeed, the Intifada erupted, at least partially,
as a response to the constant cruel oppression and brutal exploitation of the Palestinians, which was supported by the Israeli armed
forces. The Intifada was a popular demand for freedom and justice
by the Palestinians, a demand which, for at least two decades, was
rejected by the large majority of Israel's secular Jews. These nonreligious Jews placidly accepted all the so-called pragmatic reasons
why we had no choice but to live as oppressors and exploiters of a
population whose land we had occupied in a war. They thus contributed to establishing a prevailing atmosphere of mistrust of our
Palestinian neighbors, whose human and civil rights we daily
denied. Even today, you need only open a newspaper to read what
I can only call racist statements about the Palestinians, by prominent secular journalists like Shmuel Shnitzer, who was recently

awarded the Israel Prize for his so-called contribution to journalism. He was later denied the prize for his racism against the
Ethiopian Jews in Israel. In such an atmosphere, Martin Buber's
call to live a life of dialogue with our Arab neighbors has fallen on
many deaf ears.

It is true that many secular Jews firmly rejected the idolatry of the
religious Jews, and its confined approach to human rights, especially the rights of women and minorities. Unfortunately, however,
in the past thirty years, many, if not most, of these Jews chose to
dance around the golden calf of contemporary capitalism, with its
cults of progress, consumerism, and financial success. Like many
admirers of pragmatism, capitalism, and progress, these dancers
rarely—if at all—dedicated themselves to the pursuit of justice.
Consequently, these secular Jews had a very paltry spiritual message to live by and to present. To borrow a phrase from Herbert
Marcuse, their existence is one-dimensional.

Let me venture a generalization, based on Buber's ontology.
Today, the daily life of probably the majority of secular Jews is dominated and wholly taken up by relations to the It; in their daily pursuit of success, material progress, and consumerism, these Jews
strangle all opportunities of relating in dialogue to a Thou. The result is evident: Secular Jews in Israel live very much in a wasteland
of spirituality.

How can it be otherwise? When a person knows that injustices
are performed daily in one's name, or participates in performing
these injustices and does not condemn them, very often spirituality
vanishes.

Finally, I can briefly turn to the political and national level. Looking back at our history of these past thirty years, since the June 1967
War, in relation to the Palestinians, most Jews have embraced what
Buber called a nationalistic convention. We have not acted as a nation that strives to act in accordance with what Buber called its supernational goal. A supernational goal is the development of a
unique spiritual gift that a specific nation can contribute to hu-
mankind. A national goal is what certain politicians believe to be the
national interests of the nation. For us Jews in Israel, it is quite simple to point to this supernational goal. It is the daily pursuing of a
life guided by the Ten Commandments and the call for justice ex-
quisitely articulated by the Hebrew prophets. In our relations to the
Palestinians we have pretty much ignored this worthy task.

Instead of listening carefully to this supernatural task that calls out from the Bible and our history, most Jews have adopted what Buber called the abstract compulsion and the collective egoism of the nationalist convention. One example of this abstract compulsion is the decision that Hebron is a holy city, that I previously criticized. Examples of collective egoism abound, the most recent being the decision that Israel is allowed to build wherever it wants for Jews in the land surrounding Jerusalem, and all Palestinians must accept this decision placidly. Thus, from Buber's writings, we can learn that the nationalism promoted by the so-called national camp in Israel is a blatant lie. It has nothing to do with the true goals of the Jewish people, which are supernational. This fake nationalism that right-wing politicians promote is mere greed and egoism masquerading as concern for the nation; it constitutes a total denial of the supernational task that our history demands of us.

Thus, from a Buberian perspective, our relations with the Palestinians during the past thirty years can only be viewed as contributing to a period that we must contemplate with deep shame. We lost the opportunity to relate dialogically to our Palestinian neighbors, to live a genuine religious life, to undertake our supernational task as a nation. Spirituality has almost vanished from our daily lives and decisions. In their stead, blatant greed, religious idolatry, and collective egoism have become paramount and have very much characterized our relations with the Palestinians.

Can the situation change? Can it be redeemed? Only if in our everyday deeds and political actions each of us acknowledge the fact that many Israelis have sinned in relating to our neighbors. But this acknowledgment must also lead to new redeeming acts. Perhaps we can be helped in our struggle against the many crude and cruel sinners of the nationalist camp by remembering Buber's saying of more than half a century ago: "Herein lies the foulest and most fraudulent deception of all: that it is possible to achieve redemption through sin."[6]

NOTES

1. Paul R. Mendes-Flohr, *A Land of Two People: Martin Buber on Jews and Arabs* (Oxford: Oxford University Press, 1983).

2. Martin Buber, *I and Thou*, trans. Ronald Gregor Smith (New York: Scribner's, 1958), 3.

3. Ibid., 16.
4. Ibid., 49.
5. *Nekuda* 178 (May 1994): 32–35.
6. Mendes-Flohr, *A Land of Two People,* 133.

5

Comments to Haim Gordon, "A Lost Opportunity: A Buberian Outlook on the Occupation"

Paul Mendes-Flohr

In a courageously forthright manner, Haim Gordon addresses what he terms the "lost opportunities" to achieve rapprochement between Arab and Jew. The hope of forging a just pattern of relationships between the two peoples who dwell in this country—called the Land of Israel by the Jews, and Palestine by the Arabs—was born, according to Gordon, in the wake of the June 1967 War. Although Gordon does not specify what particularly about the results of that war provided this hope, presumably he means that the capture by Israeli troops of the Gaza Strip, the Golan Heights, and the West Bank brought the two populations into the same geopolitical unit, thus confronting them with the "opportunity," in Gordon's apt words, of "living justly" with one another. With a passion reflecting a deep moral concern, Gordon evokes Buber's concept of dialogue in order to explicate the nature of the "opportunity" that, alas, has been squandered.

In my reflections, I should like to highlight the political significance of Buber's doctrine of dialogue, which despite its manifest ethical overtones, as Gordon correctly points out, is not a moral doctrine per se, that is, it is not merely a code of conduct but rather a mode of being-in-the-world, and as such has, indeed, moral as well as political implications. Before proceeding, I wish to make two brief comments. The first is philological or rather semantic, namely, if in the spirit of dialogue we wish to honor Arab sensitivities, we best avoid the appellation "Six-Day War," which, while celebrating

Israeli valor and triumph, implicitly marks Arab defeat and humiliation; we thus best choose the neutral term, the June 1967 War. The
second comment is also philological, which I believe will help illuminate with swift strokes the full thrust of Gordon's argument.
Buber was wont to speak of the difference between what he called
in German, *nebeneinander* and *miteinander,* living next to one another
as opposed to living with one another. One can live next to
another—*nebeneinander*—without any morally and existentially
meaningful relationship. *Nebeneinander* characterizes much of modern life. It is the invidious ethos captured in the twentieth century
American poet Robert Frost's ironic verse, "good fences make good
neighbors." But *good* neighbors who dwell if not in harmony, at
least in mutual understanding and respect, live *miteinander* with
one another. The clarification of what living with one another—
miteinander as opposed merely to *nebeneinander*—is the burden of
Buber's teachings. He was aware, as we all are, that it is far easier
simply to set up fences demarcating one's claims, property, position, space; these fences allow us to ignore, or to encounter our
neighbors at the most in an instrumental manner. But fences, which
take many subtle shapes, mental as well as of concrete and barbed
wire, also separate neighbors by creating mutual estrangement, sus-
picion, envy, fear, antagonism.

Yet, as Buber tirelessly noted, to remove the fences and to live
with one another entails great difficulty, indeed, many risks. In an
effort to live with another, without the protection of fences, we are
at risk that our neighbor might abuse our openness. Hence, Buber
prudently spoke of mismeetings (*Vergegnungen,* in his inimitable
German). But, without the risk, the fearful divide between neighbors—the walls of fear, misunderstanding, and mistrust that are
seeds of hatred and conflict—will persist. The life of dialogue, the
life of *miteinander,* as Buber put it, is to walk a "narrow ridge." But it
is only by mustering the courage to cross that ridge can we humans
reach the full promise of life both for ourselves and our neighbors.
It is this promise that Gordon has in mind when he speaks of the opportunities engendered by the June 1967 War.

I share Gordon's assessment that the legacy of that war has been
one of a lost opportunity. The tragically missed opportunity to establish a humane and just grammar of interpersonal and intercom-
munal relations between Israeli Jews and Palestinians is not only
the moral and religious travesty that Gordon so poignantly depicts.
The failure of Jew and Arab to live *miteinander* also has grave polit-

ical consequences. To be sure, as Buber acknowledged, dialogue is not a substitute for politics, even what for the sake of shorthand we may call the politics of peace. He actually appreciated the fact that the attainment of, what again for the sake of shorthand we may call, a genuine, just peace, is perforce a complex procedure of balancing conflicting interests, needs, and hopes. In the theological language that Buber would often use, in an unredeemed—imperfect—world, emotional and material conflict is inevitable. The question is how the conflict is resolved. Fences are one way. Some believe the higher and wider those fences are is the path of political realism. Here is where Buber demurred. The security those fences provide, he believed, is ultimately chimerical. In time, all such fences crumble, their foundations undermined by the persistent presence of the Other they seek to keep out. The Other may be kept at bay for a time, a decade, a century and more, but inevitably the fence will be penetrated, especially if it is maintained at the expense of the dignity and self-esteem of the Other. Pain flusters even across generations. It is as resilient as hope.

The fences that separate peoples, Buber concluded, therefore, must be removed—but how? They can be dismantled neither by political fiat nor moral appeal. After all, the fences, as Buber well realized, are often erected for compelling existential reasons. These reasons, he claimed, can be summarized with one word, mistrust (*Mistrauen*). The loss of a primal trust—the "inborn Thou"—afflicts all beings as they gradually encounter the often harsh realities of life. Our task as humans, Buber claims, is to help each other retrieve that lost trust in the world. The difficulty of the task is graphically captured by an image employed by the philosopher and psychiatrist Karl Jaspers, when he speaks of human beings as seeking to protect themselves from each other, by building *Gehauses*, little shelters such as the shells that snails carry on their backs. It is only with the greatest of caution that a snail emerges from its shell, its *Gehause*. Stretching out its neck, it prudently checks out the terrain to ascertain whether any trouble awaits it. And should there be the slightest hint of danger, it quickly retreats into its *Gehause*, seeking protection from the brutalities of the world beyond its mobile shelter. All human beings, individually and collectively, have their *Gehause*; we can, of course, only meet each other, and forge bonds of friendship and love, if we dare exit our *Gehause*. If we are interested in the friendship and love of another, then, we must prompt the trust assuring him or her that it is safe to get out beyond his or her protective shield.

For Buber, dialogue—as Gordon has well explicated it, attentive listening to others, their stories, their fears, pain, joy, indeed, listening to the very core of their being—is a method to nurture such trust. Most such dialogues are asymmetrical, however. One partner in the prospective dialogue may be stronger—stronger emotionally, politically, socially. Some dialogues are structurally asymmetrical, such as between a teacher and a student; other dialogues are asymmetrical by force of circumstance, such as when one partner stands on the high ground of a victory, and the other is below. To initiate a dialogue, to create the first steps toward mutual trust, is thus clearly the obligation of the stronger partner. The attainment of full trust, and hence a firm and enduring dialogue is the goal. And here it is crucial to note that, for Buber, dialogue is both a method and a goal. The apparent tautology—dialogue is pre-sumed in order to be eventually attained—perhaps makes better sense to one familiar with the dynamic of faith in which one affirms a transcendent reality that is yet to be. Indeed, dialogue is a posture of faith, but a faith without which there is no hope of overcoming the mistrust that divides human beings and lays the seeds of fear and enmity. In this respect, dialogue is a meta-political principle: it both illuminates the horizons beyond conflict and outlines the path to reach that sublime destination.

To conclude these adumbrative reflections, I should like to cite an exchange between Martin Buber and a senior Egyptian diplomat, Tahseen Basheer. As a member of the Egyptian mission to the United Nations, he met Buber during the philosopher's visit to New York City in 1957. They spoke for hours. Basheer reports:

I was young and brash, he [Buber] was old and picked his words very wisely. It was a painful meeting. I said, "You've taken the land because you are stronger and have Western support. The Palestinians lost because they were weaker. Now you talk of morality but it is the morality of power. Either offer a bigger cake so as to make your presence beneficial to the other side and in time the pain will be seen as a passing phase, or give them some kind of compensation. But you do neither."

He didn't dodge the issues. I like his empathy with the Palestinians. He was pained by the problem and had no solution. At the end he said, "This was a difficult meeting and I'm going to give you a present. I'm going to tell you a hasidic story."

The story was about a young man going to a rabbi and asking him how to rid the world of evil so to permit good to enter. The rabbi's response was to just begin doing good in anticipation that evil would then subside by itself.[1]

Tahseen Basheer, who served as Gamal Nasser's spokesman at the time of the June 1967 War, adds with reference to contemporary realities, "My greatest fear is apathy among young Israelis and despair among young Palestinians." Concurring, I thus add my voice to Haim Gordon's by underscoring that dialogue is our only hope.

NOTE

1. Cited in Tahseen Basheer, "View from the Nile," interview by Abraham Rabinovich, *Jerusalem Post*, 6 June 1997, p. 9.

6

The Links Between the Israeli and Palestinian Economies Since 1967: Between Imposed Integration and Voluntary Separation

Aryeh Arnon

INTRODUCTION

For several years I have been involved in different research projects on the Palestinian economy in the West Bank and the Gaza Strip that gave me the opportunity to work with Israeli and Palestinian economists to discuss the past and to contemplate the future. Some of these efforts will appear in a forthcoming book compiled by economists from Ben-Gurion University. This chapter draws heavily on these and other collective efforts.

It is clear to those who studied the Palestinian economy that the single most important fact that determined the course of events since 1967 was the peculiar links with Israel and Israeli policy within the Occupied Territories. The links, as well as other economic policies, were shaped unilaterally by Israel according to Israeli considerations as they were conceived by Israeli policy makers. In what follows, I partially describe the role economists played in determining the links in 1967, and again in the 1990s, before and after Oslo. I also discuss the economic performances that followed in the West Bank and the Gaza Strip.

Imposed integration and voluntary separation are two extreme forms of the possible links between the Israeli and Palestinian economies. Voluntary as opposed to imposed integration, or imposed, as opposed to voluntary separation, were, of course, two

other possibilities. I will argue that Israel imposed (impure) economic integration after the June 1967 War, an economic regime that
continued with minor changes up to 1994. In 1994, following the
Declaration of Principles (DOP or Oslo I) signed between Israel and
the PLO in September 1993, an agreement between the PLO and Israel concerning the economic links was reached in Paris (the Economic Protocol), and became the de jure regime since then. Though,
as I argue below, in spite of the two sides signing the agreements,
the Paris Protocol was closer to an imposed integration regime than
to a voluntary one. Thus, the last thirty years were characterized by
what I term imposed integration.

The Paris Protocol was intended to bring prosperity to the Palestinian economy. Paradoxically, however, since the Paris agreement,
the economy suffered a severe crisis, due to the Israeli closure policy and changes in the Israeli labor market, particularly concerning
"guest laborers." For the first time since 1967, the de facto regime
(though not the de jure one) was moving in the direction of imposed
separation. The economic crisis in the West Bank and the Gaza Strip,
for which I provide recently published figures, was the result of this
new policy. I conclude with a brief discussion of the alternatives for
the future. I begin with the formative years after 1967 when economic policy was being shaped.

ECONOMIC POLICY AFTER 1967

It took about two years for the economic links between Israel and
the Palestinian economy to take shape. Two closely related elements in these links—labor and trade—had begun to take form
and led to what can be described as imposed, impure, economic integration. The interdependence of decisions regarding trade and
labor was due to the fact that together they determined the welfare
of the Palestinians. A decision to continue the total separation between both economies and Israel, as before the June 1967 War, that
is, to leave both the border for labor and the border for goods
closed, would have led to a deterioration of economic life and a
sharp drop in the standard of living. Such a strategy was not acceptable either to the Israeli government or to the military, since it
would have led to unrest and raised the cost of maintaining the status quo. Thus, either the border for labor, or that for goods, or both,
had to be opened.

Immediately after the June 1967 War, Israeli economists assessed various alternatives. The most elaborate study was prepared by a team headed by Professor Michael Bruno. The team recommended implementing the (relatively) free movement of goods, but not of factors of production, and specifically not of labor.[1] The team calculated that from an economic point of view, maintaining Israel's hold on the Palestinian territories would not be too heavy a burden on the Israeli economy. The team also addressed the question of means to encourage emigration from the territories, especially from the Gaza area. It should be emphasized that the analysis was short-term, and depended on the "political future of the territories." However, in the next eighteen months, the Israeli government adopted a different policy concerning the links: open borders for both labor and trade, with some restrictions concerning trade, mainly in agricultural goods. The reason for these restrictions was clear: to protect Israeli agriculture.

Israeli policy was shaped in a series of hidden and more public debates. Two opposing views of the links between the Israeli and Palestinian economies prevailed in the Israeli government and public. One, advocated by Defense Minister Moshe Dayan, argued for the free movement of both labor and goods. The other, presented by Finance Minister Pinhas Sapir, rejected the abolition of the labor border. The government realized that military control over the Palestinian territories would take on a "semi-permanent" form. Dayan stated his "integrationist" views in a speech in Beer Sheva in November 1968, where he favored integration of the two economies and explained that the Hebron–Beer Sheva area, on either side of the pre-1967 border, should become a single economic unit. The pro-integration camp provided short-term, practical, arguments and long-term, more principled, ones. The practical arguments related to the economic well-being of the Palestinian population, and its influence on military control: the better-off the population, the easier it would be to control. The most effective methods for raising standards of living, argued the pro-integration camp, was work in Israel. The long-term arguments were different: Dayan explained that "better acquaintance," "daily interaction," "living together," and so forth would reduce hostility and create favorable conditions for coexistence and maybe even peace in the future.

The next round in the debate, several months later, raised the issue of employment in the territories versus work in Israel. The Ministerial Committee for the Territories had to set its priorities: to create employment opportunities in the territories themselves, by encouraging the creation of new plants, by Israelis or Palestinians, versus opening the gates to work in Israel (Gazit 1985, 110–19, 147–50). Dayan, for pragmatic reasons, supported the second option; the majority, including the new prime minister, Golda Meir, favored the former. However, in spite of the majority view, no practical steps were taken to implement it.

Economic reality in the territories was stronger than all the decisions. Since no decision was made on investments in the territories, and Israeli entrepreneurs were excluded from the territories, no power could have prevented the growing phenomenon of work in Israel. At the time of the debate in the Ministerial Committee there were 15,000 workers from the territories in Israel, soon the number rose to 60,000 and maybe 70,000. (Gazit 1985, 150; author's translation)

Thus, although the documentation of the process of decision making by Israel is far from complete, the facts are clear. Integration took place, and as we will see, was almost complete by 1972. It was, however, a peculiar form of integration. First, it was involuntary. Second, it was partial in two respects: a protectionist policy biased in favor of Israeli agricultural goods, and more important, restrictions on enterpreneurship within the territories.

One of the first decisions made by the military authorities in the Palestinian territories was to allow exports of agricultural produce to Jordan. This was made possible because Dayan had managed to keep the bridges over the Jordan River open, with the Jordanian government's consent (Gazit 1985). This was known as the "open bridges policy" and created an outlet for both agricultural produce and the movement of other goods and people. The excess supply of agricultural goods in the territories, however, caused concern among Israeli farmers. As a consequence, the Israeli government provided them with protectionist policies. For several years, restrictions in the form of trade barriers prevented Palestinian agriculture from competing in the Israeli market. These barriers were later replaced by a system of quotas on various crops. Thus, instead of barriers at the "green line" (the pre-1967 borders), protectionist policies were effective at the production level.

Protectionist policies were also later applied in other sectors. A well-known example dating from 1968 was a plastic-sandals plant in Nablus. Although it was going to compete with an Israeli plant, the officer responsible for licensing imports approved a request to import the necessary machinery. The Committee of General Directors of Ministerial Offices, however, which was responsible for implementing policy in the territories, banned marketing the Nablus sandals in Israel. The case was discussed several times in various government forums, where the "separationists" advocated more restrictions and the "integrationists" favored fewer restrictions.[2] In 1972, the case was finally decided when marketing quotas were lifted and measures restricting production capacity were introduced (Gazit 1985, 261–66). Gazit summaries the policy and its consequences as follows:

Israeli policy in the administered territories created a peculiar combination of economic welfare and rising standards of living for individuals . . . combined with . . . no development within the territories themselves . . . The Israeli authorities and the military government did almost nothing to develop the local economic infrastructure (apart from the modernization of local agriculture). (Gazit 1985, 266)

The military governors and the coordinators of government activities in the territories represented the sole authority in the West Bank and Gaza. They consulted with the local Palestinian leadership on minor issues, but policy was determined by Israel. The imposed nature of the arrangements and especially the form taken by the links between the two economies were decided in Israel. Thus, characterizing the economic arrangements as imposed (partial) integration, is confirmed by the facts.

The Palestinian public sector was also controlled by Israel. Israeli officers were responsible for all facets of life, although lower-echelon civil servants remained in office under Israeli supervision. Taxes were collected and expenditures made by the newly formed public sector, although some services, notably education and health, were run mainly by Palestinians. The financial sector had ground to a virtual halt: banks had been closed in 1967 and the political instability combined with unfavorable economic conditions contributed to an undeveloped financial system.

Economic conditions in Israel immediately after the June 1967 War assisted the pro-integration camp. Israel was recovering from the 1966–1967 recession and the demand for workers increased. It is worth mentioning that the Bruno committee foresaw such events already in September 1967. In the last chapter of the report, the team of economists assessed "Changes in the Assumptions." Their discussion clearly reveals that the general assumption adopted seemed appropriate under the conditions prevailing in the economy at the time (Israel was running unemployment rates in excess of 11 percent in 1966–1967). However, the team was aware that economic conditions in Israel could change:

Concerning the near future, the prevention of work in Israel seems to be the preferred policy, based on the hypothesis that conditions in the labor market will continue to indicate a slack. However, under conditions of full employment and excess demand in the labor market, and when there are pressures on the wage rate, there is room for selective permissions to movements of Arab laborers. (Bruno Committee, 1967, chapter H, p. 2; author's translation)

The lesson is clear. The decisions on the links between the Israeli and Palestinian economies were made by Israelis according to what they perceived as Israeli interests at each point in time. Some of the major consequences for the Palestinian economy are summarized in Tables 6.1 and 6.2.

Table 6.1
Economic Data on the West Bank 1968–1993

	GNP (% annual change average)	Population (% annual change average)	Employed in Israel (% of Total Employment)	Factor Income from Abroad (% of GDP)
1968–1972	22.8	2.0	21*	20
1973–1979	5.7	1.8	30	32
1980–1987	5.0	2.4	32	28
1989–1993	9.0	4.3	31	30

*Average 1970–1972.

Source: CBS (Israel Central Bureau of Statistics), 1996.

Table 6.2
Economic Data on the Gaza Strip 1968–1993

	GNP (% annual change average)	Population (% annual change average)	Employed in Israel (% of Total Employment)	Factor Income from Abroad (% of GDP)
1968–1972	21.3	2.1	17*	9
1973–1979	8.4	2.1	37	28
1980–1987	5.4	3.0	45	57
1989–1993	7.3	5.2	34	46

*Average 1970–1972.

Source: CBS (Israel Central Bureau of Statistics), 1996.

ECONOMIC TRENDS, 1968–1994

The economic links between Israel and the Palestinian economy in the West Bank and the Gaza Strip described above resulted in an adaptation period of about five years. Many Palestinian workers left the local labor market and joined the Israeli market, where wages were higher. This process pushed up the standard of living, as measured by Gross National Product (GNP) quite rapidly during the adaptation period. After 1972, the proportion of employees working in Israel out of the total labor force reached about 30 percent in the West Bank and close to 40 percent in the Gaza Strip and remained relatively stable in the following years. The income of these workers became a significant part of disposable income. In the West Bank, remittances, also known as Factor Income from Abroad, was about 30 percent of Gross Domestic Product (GDP) and in the Gaza Strip the ratio was even higher (see Tables 6.1 and 6.2).

The balance of trade of the Palestinian economy revealed another form of dependency: the imposed and peculiar type of economic integration between the Israeli and Palestinian economies resulted in structural imbalances, and more specifically, in very low levels of exports (excluding labor services) and high levels of imports. Trade with Israel far exceeded trade with other partners. The trade deficit was paid for mainly by labor in Israel, but also through transfers from abroad and capital flows. The systematic imbalances cannot be explained simply by pure economic forces; they are the result of noneconomic factors as well. These noneconomic factors, which contributed to the asymmetric relations between Israel and the Palestinian economy, are often termed "administrative measures" or "political intervention" in the otherwise pure or autonomous economic process.

The trade regime that has existed between Israel and the Palestinian economy since 1967 is best described as an *involuntary, one-sided, impure, customs union.* Exchange between Israeli and Palestinian traders was ostensibly free and the geographical area comprising Israel, and the West Bank, and Gaza Strip had no internal trade borders, or trade barriers.[3] Trade with the rest of the world was carried out under the Israeli trade regime and according to Israel's (changing) policies. Thus, Israeli customs and other barriers to trade operated along the external borders of the combined area. Since there was no Palestinian (economic) authority and Palestinians did not participate in policy making, all decisions were made by the Israeli authorities.

In theory , such a one-sided customs union should have resulted in different economic processes from those that actually evolved. Thus, in spite of the asymmetrical trade regime, the difference in real wages between Israel and the Palestinian economy should have led to more Palestinian goods being sold on the Israeli market, and less Israeli goods being sold on the Palestinian market. The fact that this did not happen was the result of political causes or intervention in the economic process. One major kind of intervention took the form of direct administrative measures related to production capacity in the Palestinian economy. Palestinian entrepreneurs had to apply for licenses from the Israeli authorities for every economic activity they sought to initiate. Israel's policy, at least until the 1990s, was not to encourage local economic development.[4] This policy, and the measures taken to enforce it, turned important sections of the Palestinian market into a captive market in which Israeli producers had a significant advantage, and put the Israeli market almost out of reach of potential Palestinian entrepreneurs who would otherwise have been able to compete with Israeli and foreign producers. Under the economic circumstances that prevailed between 1968 and 1994, when imposed economic integration was in force, theory would have led us to predict the emergence of tough competition between Israeli and Palestinian producers in both markets. Such competition never materialized.

After the outbreak of the Intifada in December 1987, when it became clear to some observers—including some Israeli officials—that the structure of the links between the Israeli and Palestinian economies needed urgent reevaluation, Defense Minister Arens appointed a committee charged with "examining means to develop the economy of the Gaza Strip." The Sadan Committee,[5] chaired by Professor Ezra Sadan of Hebrew University, reviewed the alternatives, and emphasized the need to retain a "common market" approach. The committee stated clearly, however, that the common market framework had been only partly implemented, and that the time had come to modify the links between the Gaza Strip economy and Israel in order to change the former's extreme dependence on work in Israel into an emphasis on the export of goods. The reevaluation of Israeli economic policy in the Palestinian territories led the committee to one of the most revealing statements about the policy of Israel towards the Palestinian economy:

All the governments of Israel recognized their obligation to care for the welfare of the inhabitants of the Gaza Strip. However, in advancing the economic interests of the population the focus was on wage earners and on the short run. As regards wage earners, priority was given to increasing their income by employing them in the [Israeli] . . . economy. Only rarely did the policy opt for the development of infrastructure and encouraging the creation of factories and employment within the [Gaza Strip] itself (e.g., the creation of the Erez industrial zone). No priority was given to *the advancement of local entrepreneurship and the business sector* in the Gaza Strip. Moreover, the authorities frustrated such initiatives whenever they threatened to compete in the Israeli market with existing Israeli firms. [(Sadan 1991), author's translation; italics in original]

This is rare official acknowledgment that the policy implemented since 1967, both in the Gaza Strip and in the West Bank, was not in the best interests of the Palestinian economy. Policy was shaped by Israelis, in their best interests, as the authorities perceived them. Not only did the authorities fail to encourage the Palestinian economy, they created obstacles aimed at protecting particular Israeli interests. The Sadan Committee recommended a change in policy that would "allow and encourage initiatives in the Gaza Strip *including those that compete with Israeli products.*" (Sadan Committee, 1991, italics in the original; author's translation).

The penetration of Palestinian products into the Israeli market faced not only traditional barriers to trade (though not in the form of customs but rather as regulations and standards governing the passage of goods from one economy to the other), but also barriers to the production of goods. As a result, competition between Palestinian and Israeli producers, in both the Palestinian and the Israeli markets, was severely restricted by noneconomic forces. These restrictions help explain some of the peculiarities of the structure of trade.

THE IMPOSED INTEGRATION SHATTERED

In December 1987, more than twenty years after Israel occupied the West Bank and the Gaza Strip, a major popular uprising erupted, known as the Intifada, with important political and economic ramifications. Since then, the links between the Israeli and Palestinian economies, as briefly described, were shattered, and people on both sides set out on a serious search for alternatives. The search was mainly conducted in the political sphere, but the economic dimension also received some attention.

The PLO's decision of November 1988, in Algiers, to accept a "two state" solution to the conflict, along with other international, global, and regional changes (such as the collapse of the USSR in 1989 and the Gulf War in 1991), opened a "window of opportunity." This resulted in the Madrid Conference (October 1991), and later, with the change of government in Israel, in the signing of the Declaration of Principles (DOP) in Oslo in September 1993. These major political developments were reflected in the Palestinian economy and in its links with the Israeli economy. The DOP stipulated the schedule for the peace process: first, an interim agreement, followed by a permanent settlement of the Palestinian-Israeli conflict. With regard to economic arrangements, the most dramatic change was the mutual recognition that there were two legitimate parties to every economic decision affecting the Palestinian economy.

After several months of negotiations, the Israeli government and the PLO reached a political and economic agreement concerning the implementation of the DOP. In its first phase, this agreement included handing over the areas of the Gaza Strip and the city of Jericho in the West Bank to the Palestinian Authority. Later, the economic agreement, known as the Paris Protocol,[6] turned the de facto, imposed arrangements into agreed-upon ones. Caution should be exercised in referring to the arrangements as "voluntary," since some duress can exist even when two sides sign an agreement. However, the analysis of such an agreement, and the reasons why the parties accepted them, are totally different from the unilateral arrangements that were in place up to this point. The Protocol declared that from that point on, Israel was not responsible alone for economic policy, but that the Palestinians would decide their preferred policy.

The Protocol, which preserved the customs union and the open-borders policy on labor, was extended during the last months of 1995 from the Gaza Strip and Jericho to other cities and villages in the West Bank, which came under the jurisdiction of the Palestinian Authority. The elections to the Palestinian Council on January 20, 1996, created an elected authority that, for the first time, had a say on economic matters. However, the Protocol's basic approach to economic issues, and especially its position vis-à-vis the links between the Israeli and Palestinian economies, was not implemented. Since May 1994, a spate of violent attacks by Palestinians within Israel proper, and the resultant public outcry led to a series of closures of the Gaza Strip and the West Bank, which turned the free movement of goods and labor into dead letter. Since several Israeli industries depended on Palestinian labor, it is not surprising that it took some time for these industries (especially construction and agriculture) to adapt to the new circumstances. One of the factors that made it easier for them to adapt was the growing flood of foreign laborers to Israel: from 10,000 in February 1994, just before the signing of the *Protocol,* to around 200,000 two years later.

Thus, today, after almost thirty years of Israeli rule, the imposed integration is collapsing.

ECONOMIC PERFORMANCE, 1993–1996

The data on this period suffer from many weaknesses, partly due to the fact that the Israeli Central Bureau of Statistics stopped collecting data just as the Palestinian Central Bureau of Statistics (PCBS) started to function. The data for this time period are based on PCBS and international organizations such as the International Monetary Fund (IMF) and the World Bank. After 1993, the ratio of Palestinian workers who found employment in the Israeli economy out of the total number of those employed decreased dramatically: from 16 percent in 1994 to only 7 percent in 1996 for the West Bank and the Gaza Strip (see Tables 6.2 and 6.3). The income received for work in Israel, and the Factor Income from Abroad, declined from

Table 6.3
Economic Data on the West Bank and Gaza Strip 1993–1996 (%)

	GNP (% annual change average)	Population (% annual change average)	Employed in Israel (% of Total Employment)	Factor Income from Abroad (% of GDP)	Unemployment
1993	–10	4.5	26	18	18
1994	4	6	16	11	25
1995	–2.5*	6.8	9	7	29
1996	–3.0*	6	7	6	34

*Estimates

Source: IMF, PCBS, and the World Bank.

its past peak of more than 40 percent of GDP to 11 percent in 1994 and 6 percent in 1996. The major causes for these structural changes in the links between the Israeli and Palestinian economies were the new closure policy that Israel introduced in 1993, and the related influx of foreign laborers to the Israeli economy. These two processes placed the Israeli economy beyond the reach of many Palestinian workers, particularly in the Gaza Strip.

The closures also had a negative impact on trade relations, and as a result, unemployment in the West Bank and Gaza Strip reached unprecedented levels: 25 percent in 1994 and 34 percent in 1996. The result of the new economic links was a sharp decline in standards of living. GNP per capita fell from 1992 to 1996 by about 35 percent.

SOME COMMENTS ABOUT THE FUTURE

What are the alternatives? One must first distinguish between the short and the long term. In the next few years, before a permanent agreement is signed, some urgent modifications in the Paris Protocol are necessary. The Palestinian economy should have better access to foreign markets and labor mobility should be less dependent on changing political occurrences.

Later, once permanent agreements are negotiated, the options open to the negotiators can be defined in terms of the permeability of the economic borders and the degree of independence in economic policy-making. Thus, the labor border can be, in principle, "open," for instance, non-existent, or blocked, or, more realistically, shaped as an economic filter, where the parties to the agreements specify rules concerning labor movements. These rules will define the entry of Palestinian laborers into the Israeli economy and vice versa. The agreements will specify the terms for entering the other side's labor market, and will relate to both employers' and employees' rights and obligations. The 1994 Paris Economic Protocol is a good example of such an arrangement. The lessons of the period which elapsed since that agreement was signed, point to the close link between each side's internal economic policies and the other side's macroeconomic environment. Thus, while the negotiators in 1994 assumed that more than one hundred thousand Palestinian workers would be employed in the Israeli economy, the closure policy, and even more important, the new Israeli policy regarding foreign laborers, made this assumption unrealistic. Access to the Israeli labor market depends not only on the penetrability of the labor borders, but on the demand for Palestinian laborers within Israel. Is this an internal Israeli policy issue or a legitimate part of the negotiations?

Trade borders, too, can be "non-existent," "blocked," or serve as an economic filter that will let goods pass through according to rules agreed-upon by the two partners. The 1994 agreements assumed, in principle, no trade borders between the Palestinian and Israeli economies, and a joint border between the combined areas of the two entities with respect to the rest of the world. The latter was shaped unilaterally by Israel, and agreements on revenue sharing were incomplete. What the period since the signing of the agreements revealed was that trade barriers were, in fact, created. The two sides interpreted the creation of these barriers quite differently. Israel attributed the barriers to security concerns, caused by the continuation of violent attacks within Israel; the Palestinians perceived the new barriers as a form of collective punishment. The assumption of the 1994 agreements, that no borders would exist, caused many difficulties in monitoring movements of trade and labor, and resulted in more severe obstacles to the movement of trade and labor than arrangements that would have negotiated the existence of economic borders.

The lessons for a new development strategy that take into account the political realities of the region are clear: the Palestinian economy cannot and should not rely on employment in Israel as the main solution to excess supply in the labor market. Emphasis should be on the creation of employment opportunities within the Palestinian economy. Such might create short-term costs, but the long-term benefits seem to justify such a strategy. Hence, the creation of stable economic conditions and a clearly defined legal and commercial environment are a top priority. The roles of the private and public sectors should become clear to potential participants in the development effort.

The trade regime should reflect and encourage this new strategy. Trade relations should be nondiscriminatory. Israeli products should have equal access to the Palestinian economy and enjoy a "Most Favored Nation" status. At the same time, trade relations can be asymmetrical: Israel could and perhaps should provide the Palestinian economy with preferential treatment. This treatment would be similar to that granted Israel by the European Union in the past. It might seem costly to Israel in the short run, but it is beneficial in the long run.

The political process of achieving reconciliation might encounter difficulties. The fact of living together on the same tract of land forces both sides to reach arrangements that will address the other side's interests as well as its own. Economic cooperation in production and trade must create win-win arrangements that will be viable for both societies that live so much closer to each other than is realized today.

Thus, a "Filters Plan" can provide an answer for permanent future arrangements. Such a plan will be feasible only if the parties agree on the demarcation of specific economic borders and the arrangements along them. The agreement will have to specify what can and what cannot cross these borders, and to stipulate the specific arrangements concerning the passage of goods and labor. The agreement should be such that under no circumstances will the borders be closed for more than brief periods. Border-crossing procedures should be sophisticated enough to enable satisfactory security checks. The alternative to such a plan is the complete separation of the Palestinian economy from Israel, with all the consequences that such entails for the welfare and potential growth of the Palestinian economy.

The illusion of a possible leap from an imposed integration to a voluntary one has gradually evaporated. For both political and economic reasons, a permanent agreement will necessitate borders between the Israeli and Palestinian economies. In order to create conditions conducive to growth and welfare, the borders need to remain as open as possible under all circumstances. This might seem inferior to the no-borders solution advocated by most international agencies and experts,[7] but I believe that this is another example of where second best is a realistic solution. Those who believe that a common market, or complete economic integration, is a better solution, will have to wait for the political circumstances to change.

NOTES

1. The team submitted its report in September 1967. Its members included well-known Israeli economists such as Yoram Ben-Porath, Haim Ben-Shahar, Nadav Halevi, Giora Hanoch, Ezra Sadan, and Eitan Berglas.

2. In addition to Finance Minister Pinhas Sapir, a known participant in the debate was Deputy Prime Minister Yigal Alon, who demanded that every proposal to build a plant employing more than twenty persons, or with capital of more than (approximately) $20,000, should be brought before a Committee of General Directors (Gazit, 1985, 112).

3. There were certain exceptions.

4. The study of Israel's economic policy regarding the West Bank and Gaza Strip suffers from a paucity of reliable sources. However, the written evidence of retired high-ranking officials (Gazit, 1985) and the report of the Sadan Committee (1991), which recommended changing Israel's policy towards the Gaza Strip economy, support the claims made in the text.

5. The Sadan Committee included, among other experts, General Danny Rothshild (coordinator of government activity in the territories at the time) and Amos Rubin (economic adviser to the prime minister).

6. The *Protocol on Economic Relations between the Government of the State of Israel and the PLO, representing the Palestinian people* was signed in Paris on April 29, 1994. It became part of the Gaza-Jericho agreement signed in Cairo on May 5, 1994.

7. See World Bank (1993); Ben-Shahar Committee and the Protocol itself.

SELECTED BIBLIOGRAPHY

Arnon, A., and D. Gottlieb. 1995. "A Macroeconomic Model of the Palestinian Economy: The West Bank and the Gaza Strip 1968–1991." *Bank of Israel Review* 69:49–73.

Arnon, A., with I. Luski, A. Spivak, and J. Weinblatt. Forthcoming. *The Palestinian Economy: Between Imposed Integration and Voluntary Separation.* Leiden: Brill.

Arnon, A., and A. Spivak. 1996. "A Seigniorage Perspective on the Introduction of a Palestinian Currency." *Middle East Business and Eco-*

nomic Review 8(1):1–14. (Also Discussion Paper 95.04, Research Department, Bank of Israel.)

Arnon, A., A. Spivak, and J. Weinblatt. 1996. "The Potential for Trade Between Israel, the Palestinians and Jordan." *The World Economy*
19:113–34.

Ben-Shahar, H. 1993. *Report of the Economic Consulting Team to the Political
Negotiations* (in Hebrew).

Bruno, M. 1967. *Report of Committee on the Development of the Administered
Territories, Team for Economic-Social Planning* (in Hebrew).

CBS (Israel Central Bureau of Statistics). 1996. *National Accounts of the Judea,
Samaria and the Gaza Area 1968–1993*. Special Report No. 1012.
Jerusalem.

Elmusa, S., and M. El-Jafari. 1995. "Power and Trade: The Israeli-Palestinian Economic Protocol." *Journal of Palestine Studies* 24:14–32.

Fischer, S., D. Rodrik, and E. Tuma, eds. 1993. *The Economics of Middle East
Peace: Views from the Region*. Cambridge, MA: MIT Press.

Gazit, S. 1985. *The Carrot and the Stick: Israel's Policy in Judea and Samaria,
1967–1968* (in Hebrew). Tel Aviv: Zmora-Bitan; also in English:
1995. Washington, DC: B'nai B'rith Books.

Hawed O. A., and R. A. Shaban. 1993. "One-Sided Customs and Monetary
Union: The Case of the West Bank and Gaza Strip under Israeli Occupation." In Fischer et al. (1993), 117–48.

Kleiman, E. 1993. "Some Basic Problems of the Economic Relationships between Israel, and the West Bank, and Gaza." In Fischer et al. 1993.

Meyshar, Y. 1994. "On the Desirability of Proper Borders between Israel
and the Palestinian Entity: Economics and Politics Overshadowed
by Sociology and Demographics" (in Hebrew). *The Economic Quarterly* 41(4):656–74.

Palestine Central Bureau of Statistics. 1996a. *Demographic Survey 1995*.
———. 1996b. *Labour Force Survey*.

*Protocol on Economic Relations between the Government of the State of Israel and
the PLO, representing the Palestinian people*, Paris, 1994.

Sadan, E. 1991. *Interim Report of the Committee on the Gaza Area* (Hebrew).

Shaban R. A. 1993. "Palestinian Labour Mobility." *International Labour Review* 132:655–72.

United Nations Office of the Special Coordinator in the Occupied Territories. 1997. *Economic and Social Conditions in the West Bank and Gaza
Strip*. Gaza.

World Bank. 1993. *Developing the Occupied Territories: An Investment in
Peace*. 6 vols. Washington, DC: The World Bank.

7

Breaking the Mirror—Oslo and After

Ilan Pappe

OSLO THE DOCUMENT AND OSLO THE PROCESS

By now it is clear that one should distinguish between the Oslo agreement the document, or the plan, and the Oslo accord as a reality or as a process. The Oslo plan was devised by Israelis belonging to the Zionist left, members of the Labor movement, who had a mandate to extend beyond that movement's traditional positions and seek an agreement with the PLO based on a solution acceptable to the Zionist parties, left of the Labor movement. These negotiators met a group of pragmatic members from the PLO's second echelon, seated at the time at Tunis. The Palestinian negotiators came to Oslo on the basis of the resolutions adopted by the Palestinian National Council's (PNC) 18th convention accepting the principle of partition as the basis for a solution to the conflict.[1] The principle of partition recognized the inability of the PLO to force an agreement based on the establishment of a secular Arab state in all ex-mandatory Palestine. Nonetheless, the PLO was still loyal to the Right of Return of the Palestinian refugees and committed to the establishment of a Palestinian state next to Israel, free of Jewish settlements, fully independent, with its capital Jerusalem.

However, these points were, for the first time in the PLO's history, negotiable and not just precepts of a national ideology. This new pragmatism was brought about by the disappearance of the Soviet Union as a supporting superpower of the PLO; the decrease in

Saudi financial assistance in the wake of the PLO's neutral position in the Gulf War; and the overall decline in the PLO's fortunes in the Arab world at large and in Palestine in particular, following its eviction from Lebanon in 1982. As was the case with the Declaration of Independence on November 15, 1988 (the resolutions of the 19th PNC Convention), so in 1993, this move to an agreement was also prompted by the success of the Intifada to attract public support inside and outside Palestine on a level and intensity unattained in the past by the PLO's guerrilla movement. But more than anything else, the new pragmatism was part of a long process, begun in 1974, which turned the PLO into a pragmatic actor on the Middle Eastern stage—hoping to achieve its goals, like anyone else in this area, through a mixture of force and diplomacy. Finally, one can assume that the 1992 election in Israel of a government declaring a willingness to evacuate occupied territories encouraged such negotiations as well. Thus, the Oslo document represented the meeting point between an Israeli wish to compromise territorially and a PLO readiness to begin peace negotiations, but by no means to conclude it, with such a compromise.

Despite the unfavorable background against which the PLO conducted these negotiations, and notwithstanding the superior position of Israel in the balance of power between the two sides, Oslo opened a significant window of opportunity for the leaders of the Palestinian national movement. By Oslo is meant the Declaration of Principles (DOP) proclaimed on September 13, 1993, as a binding agreement on the White House lawn. Article 5 clause 3 of the agreement promises that three subjects would be dealt with in future negotiations, after a successful implementation of an interim agreement between the two sides: the question of Jerusalem, the fate of the Palestinian refugees, and the problem of the Jewish settlements in the Occupied Territories. Additionally, clause 3 allows each party to bring to the table, pending an agreement of the other, any other topic it wishes for discussion.

The main PLO concession was to link the successful implementation of the interim period with the negotiations on the final status of the territories and these three topics. The DOP specified the nature of the interim period: an Israeli withdrawal from Gaza and Jericho, to be followed by a gradual transfer of certain civil functions from Israel to the PLO, and an eventual Israeli evacuation of all the Palestinian towns and population centers. At the end of the period, talks on the final settlement were to commence.

This interim agreement was dictated by the Israelis and tailored according to their perception of security. Moreover, it represented the Israeli conception of the conflict's nature and substance. The agreement dealt only with problems emanating from the June 1967 War, as if that year was the formative year of the conflict and everything that preceded it was irrelevant to a peaceful solution of the conflict. The interim phase contributed to ending Israeli control over the lives of a large number of Palestinians. It did not include any reference to the Palestinian perception of the conflict: it did not advance solutions for the uprooted Palestinians who had lost Palestine in 1948. This Palestinian concession was buttressed by symbols of Palestinian sovereignty in every evacuated area, the most important of which—and one that went beyond symbolism—was the recognition of the PLO's authority to rule these areas.

But more than anything else, the framework of the interim phase was tolerated by the Palestinians because of the promise given in clause 5 subclause 3 of the document. It was not only the question of refugees and Jerusalem that were important; the PLO hoped that it could also raise the issue of final statehood in future negotiations. All three issues are related to the consequences of the 1948 war; a war that constructed in many ways the national identity of the Palestinians and dictated their national agenda.[2] The PLO owes its existence to the 1948 refugee community and its raison d'être has never been to bring an end to the Israeli occupation of 1967—which was a secondary task—but to rectify the evils of 1948.

Although hidden in a subclause, these promises included in Oslo the document represent a PLO achievement. Apart from being recognized by Israel for the first time in its history, the PLO was granted an Israeli willingness to negotiate over three issues which had been regarded by the PLO as being at the heart of the conflict: the fate of the refugees, the future of Jerusalem, and the establishment of a Palestinian state. The Israelis very skillfully added to these a 1967 issue, that of the settlements, a contentious and delicate matter for the Israeli electorate. Hence, the Israelis wished to postpone negotiations concerning the settlements for as long as possible. The document stressed, however, Israel's veto power over this breakthrough: Israel conditioned its participation in such negotiations on a "successful and peaceful" implementation of the interim agreement. "Peaceful" meant in such a way that would satisfy the Israeli concept of security, hence the implementation of that phase was to be monitored and executed by Israeli generals.

Oslo on the ground, Oslo as a process, was a far cry from Oslo the document. In a series of agreements dictated by the Israeli generals, who were faced by a Palestinian team that lacked any professional expertise in legal and strategic matters, interim objectives of Oslo the document seemed to become the basis for the final and permanent settlement of the conflict.[3] A series of Israeli actions, or, if you wish, of Palestinian concessions, rendered impractical and useless any future negotiations on the issues relating to a final status of the territories or on the questions of refugees and Jerusalem.

This process has annulled some of the principal promises made in Oslo the document. For instance, Article 31 clause 7 declares: "Neither side shall initiate or take any step that will change the status of the West Bank and the Gaza Strip pending the outcome of the permanent status negotiations." Yet, from 1994 on, Israel began a construction effort, including border fences, which delineated the West Bank's partition, prior to any negotiations.

In each of the various agreements signed after Oslo, the balance of power and Israeli superiority were translated into realities of life in the supposedly negotiable areas. This was manifest in all spheres of life that enable the Israelis to gain influence through the employment of violent means: arrests, detention, house demolitions, etc. More than anything else, it appears in the continuation of the settlement policies. Massive land confiscation and settlement expansion marked the four years under the Labor government, 1992–1996. Such acts contradicted both the spirit of Oslo and an explicit pledge made by the late prime minister, Yitzhak Rabin, to freeze settlement expansion. The Labor government invested $46 million in the Jewish settlers, a population of about 144,000 people in the occupied Palestinian territories (much more than its predecessors of the Likud). By 1996, the settler population increased by 48 percent in the West Bank and 62 percent in the Gaza Strip.[4] All this has made the eviction of settlers from Palestinian areas even more unrealistic than before.

Apart from making final talks impossible, this was an additional violation of Oslo the document. Article 31 clause 8 declares that "The two parties view the West Bank and the Gaza Strip as a single territorial unit, the integrity and status of which will be preserved during the interim period." This clause was repeatedly violated by Israel. A series of bypasses and tunnels bisected the West Bank territories, creating an imagined map of a Jewish West Bank above—in more than one sense—the Palestinian one. Jews were not just living next to Palestinians, but above them, or were digging tunnels below them. The small Jewish settlements are now connected to larger ones and to Israel proper by special highways; the Palestinians living in the areas circled by blocks of settlements can only travel by passing through a series of military barriers with great difficulty, if at all. The paving of highways, the digging of tunnels, and the cantonization of the West Bank (more will be said later of the Gaza Strip), are what define Oslo the process. These arrangements derived their legitimacy not from the DOP, but from the various agreements signed by Israel and the new creation of Oslo—the Palestinian Authority (PA). Time will tell whether the PA has replaced the PLO; in the eyes of the Israelis at least, this replacement is an irreversible fact. Through agreements with the PA, Israel now has confirmation for its actions by a recognized leadership of the Palestinian national movement.

Palestinians traveling from one part of the West Bank to another, or from the areas under the PA's authority to work in Israel, could see better than anyone else the patterns of continuity between the pre- and post-Oslo realities. The misbehavior and callousness of Israeli soldiers and policemen at the many roadblocks revealed that the West Bank had turned into a Bantustan and nothing more. The occupiers were still there at the roadblocks, able to inflict any kind of mental and physical abuse on those under their hands. This is also a violation of Oslo the document, apart from being a continuation of the occupation. Article 10 clause 1, subclause a, states: "there shall be a safe passage connecting the West Bank with the Gaza Strip for movement of persons, vehicles and goods." Subclause b declares that "Israel will ensure safe passage for persons and transportation during daylight hours (from sunrise to sunset) or as otherwise agreed by the JSC [Joint Security Commission], but in any event not less than 10 hours a day." This clause was not only violated in the case of the passage between the Gaza Strip and the West Bank, but inside the West Bank as well.

The violation was manifested in the tension between parameters and functions. The Israelis control the parameters while the Palestinians control some functions. This formula is a hybrid between two old Israeli peace plans: one offered by Yigal Allon, the other by Moshe Dayan. Both were presented in the 1970s. Allon sought a territorial compromise with the Jordanians, based on the demographic distribution in the territories. Dayan suggested dividing the functions of authority between Israel and Jordan—with Israel holding mainly security functions in the West Bank and the Jordanians all the rest. These two approaches, in which the Palestinians replace the Hashemites as partners, are the basis of the current proposals of a permanent settlement offered jointly by Labor and Likud in the post-Oslo reality. But even in the field of functions, Oslo the process, did not go very far. The Palestinian functions are limited to running daily domestic life in the PA areas. They are decorated with symbols that substitute for real sovereignty: flags, units, names, and titles such as Palestine's Postal Service. It is what the Palestinians call a lot of *Salata* (honors) without *Sulta* (authority).

But this new reality not only continues past realities, it incurs new patterns of life that explain why, despite the obvious disadvantage for the Palestinians, a significant number of them living in the West Bank and the Gaza Strip were for a long time willing partners to the process. The advantages promised in the accord can be seen more vividly in Gaza. The Strip was less divided than the West Bank. Its separation from the West Bank has an accepted reality, as an arrangement that would exist for a long time, even if Oslo the document was implemented verbatim or according to a pro-PLO interpretation. It was there that at first, because of relative territorial integrity, that the removal of the direct Israeli occupation was felt. No more curfews, no more army break-ins at night, and no more harassment on the roads. It took more than a year before the repeated closures[5] and heavy restrictions of movement outside the Gaza Strip drove home the message of Oslo the process: turning the Gaza Strip into one huge prison with a Palestinian flag inside, and Israeli soldiers guarding the fences. As mentioned, the restrictions of movement were contrary to several articles in Oslo the document. They are also a violation of Article 33 of the Fourth Geneva convention of 1949, "Relative to the Protection of Civilian Persons in Time of War."

Why did Oslo the process gain such support from both sides, at least until 1996? For the Palestinians, note that the Oslo reality provided jobs for a large number of Palestinians within the various mechanisms erected to regulate life in the areas governed by the Palestinian Authority. These employers became a main body of support for the agreement with a vested interest in maintaining the status quo.

For the Israelis, Oslo was presented in the public discourse, at least until the election of Netanyahu, as a peace process. Much effort was invested by Israel to convey this message of progress. The violent hostility of the Zionist Right to Oslo strengthened the conviction of many Israelis on the Left that they were defending a genuine peace process against its enemies. And finally, in the international, and particularly the American, discourse, the Oslo accord meant peace.

QUO VADIS? POST-OSLO PALESTINE AND ISRAEL

As explained above, Oslo as a reality and as a peace process were very different from the document signed in 1993. It seems futile to question whether such was intended or if the peace process went astray. What is important is the transformation of Oslo into a form of indirect occupation, provided by an alliance between the Israeli government and sections of the Palestinian Authority. In all the agreements that meant to translate Oslo from a declaration of principles into a reality, Israel dictated an arrangement that would unnecessary render any final negotiations on a permanent solution.

This dictum is exercised by both the previous and present governments of Israel. It enjoys wide support among the Jewish population.[6] In fact, as the elections of 1996 show, the majority of Jewish voters in Israel are willing to impose the Oslo reality in even harsher conditions, the ones suggested by the Likud. It seems that this is the greatest attraction of Oslo the process for the Israelis. It appeals to the political center. Immediately after the 1996 Israeli elections, on June 4, 1996, Yossi Beilin, a leader of Labor and so-called dove, announced that he believed Labor and Likud could find a common ground for peace making.

A common platform for peace is the best way for political parties such as Likud and Labor to avoid relying too much on fringe parties. A look at the two party platforms indeed shows a considerable overlap on the question of Oslo. Labor proposes that in the final peace agreement none of the 144 Jewish settlements in the West Bank and Gaza be evacuated, and that most of them should remain under Israeli sovereignty. Labor and Likud insist that Jerusalem remain united under Israeli control. They differ on the question of statehood in their official positions, but in reality, what they both offer to the Palestinians is far from normal statehood.

The extent of the agreement within the center of the Israeli political system can be seen in the Eitan-Beilin document,[7] which intends to provide the basis for a future unity government in Israel. Beilin is supposedly on the left of the Labor party and Eitan is considered on the right of the Likud. And yet they found it quite simple to reach an agreement that would dictate to the Palestinians that almost all the Israeli settlements are to remain under Israeli control and sovereignty, Jerusalem is to be united under Israeli rule, and Israel is to be responsible for security on the Jordan River. There is no mention of any solution to the refugee problem, but there is agreement that a semblance of statehood would be given to the Palestinians in the areas that would remain under their control.

The idea of a Palestinian state first appeared in the Abu Mazin-Beilin document.[8] In February 1996, Mahmud Abas, known as Abu Mazin, negotiated secretly with Beilin. The two men presented to Arafat and then Israeli prime minister, Shimon Peres, an agreement that included recognition of a Palestinian state without an army; continued Israeli control over most of the Jewish settlers; Palestinian control over the Jordan valley beginning in the year 2007; and an expansion of Israeli municipal control in Jerusalem with some boroughs, namely Aub Dis, under Palestinian authority. This agreement, which a prominent member of the Palestinian Authority accepted, was a scheme that would make Palestine a Bantustan on less than 55 percent of the West Bank and 60 percent of the Gaza Strip, with a minicapital at Abu Dis, and without any solution for the refugee problem, and without dismantling any Jewish settlements. Thus, the Beilin-Eitan document shows that many Israelis already know what they want as a permanent settlement. Everything so far achieved by the process indeed indicates that such will be the end result of Oslo: a Bantustan under Israeli control.

However, Eitan and Beilin share another idea, which may not interest most Israelis but definitely serves as an explanation of the economic forces behind Oslo, which cut across national boundaries. Part of this vision is the introduction of a capitalist and free-market economy both in Israel and in Palestine. Under the 1994 Paris agreements, which were the economic components of Oslo, Israel and Palestine were to be one economic unit.[9] Such can be seen in the way the customs units are connected, and the way a joint taxation policy is being exercised. This unification is ensured by the decision to postpone any substantial negotiations over the introduction of a Palestinian currency. Furthermore, the agreement grants Israel the right of veto on any development scheme put forward by the PA. This means that the monetary and developmental policies of Israel and its currency exchanges are to play a dominant role in the Palestinian economy. Other aspects of the economy such as foreign trade and industry are also totally dominated by the Israelis.

The introduction of the Israeli version of a capitalist society into the Palestinian areas can only have a disastrous effect. With the absence of a democratic structure and a very low Gross National Product (GNP), such an approach toward integration, as offered by Oslo, can only turn the areas under the Palestinian Authority into the slums of Israel. An example of such a development area can already be seen near the Erez checkpoint, in the buffer zone between Israel and Gaza. There, the Israelis, with the blessing of the United States and the European Union, opened an industrial park. Let the name not mislead; it is primarily a production line where all the workers are Palestinians and the employers are Israelis who benefit from the very low wages they pay their workers. Israel has similar visions for such parks on the border with Jordan and the West Bank. No wonder many industrialists in Israel see themselves as belonging to the peace camp. This is only one aspect of the capitalization of Palestine accompanying the peace process.

While this double burden of economic misery and lack of genuine progress on the national front can lead to a Palestinian attempt to rebel against the post-Oslo reality, it is difficult to see why Israelis should make an effort to alter the current situation. For the majority of the Jewish population in Israel, this peace is based on unbeatable logic, which was repeatedly pronounced by the late prime minister, Yitzhak Rabin: the Palestinians were in a very dismal situation before Oslo, they are now offered an improvement. Not a very impressive one, but still one that can be defined as an N+1 formula. N is the previous situation, 1 is Gaza, Jericho, and Ramallah covered with Palestinian flags and guarded by Palestinian policemen. 1 is a nondemocratic authority, which replaced Israeli occupation with the Palestinian security services.

There are problems, however, on the Palestinian side. Already in 1995, Palestinian dissatisfaction with the progress of Oslo the process aroused such indignation and resistance as to endanger the whole peace process. The election of Netanyahu, despite his stated commitment to fulfill Oslo and the evacuation of Hebron (an act the Labor government did not dare to execute), has increased the level of disillusionment and nonconfidence in the peace process. In September 1996, these feelings were translated into an open uprising following the opening of a tunnel under the Temple Mount, Haram al-Sharif. Other limited uprisings followed due to the stalemate in the negotiations and Israel's settlement policies in Jerusalem.

One possible outcome of all this is the expansion of such a mini-Intifada into an overall uprising. But there seems little reason and will within the PA to embark on such a policy. The more likely scenario is that a future government in Israel will dictate a settlement to the Palestinians based on the N+1 formula, which may or may not lead to a violent eruption. We are here concerned with wider implications of the reality as it is constituted now and the fact that the Palestinians do not have the power to alter it drastically.

The final part of this chapter will examine the future of this "peace" with the help of an academic exercise inspired by political sociology. This is a theoretical attempt to present the possible trends of the post-Oslo reality by pointing to long-term processes that might eventually undermine the current picture or stalemate. This is not an apocalyptic scenario of war and violence, which are of course possible developments. Our analysis has more to do with the inadequacy of the current political structures in carrying the weight of the social and cultural fragmentation of the Israeli and Palestinian societies. This inadequacy was planted into the lives of Jews and Palestinians long before Oslo. It had been part of the political structure imposed on the eastern Mediterranean by the mandatory powers after World War I; it was altered by the consequences of the 1948 war and was altered again in the wake of the June 1967 War. The inadequacy emerges in an ever-growing tension between the formations and nature of the state and the social and cultural fabric of the societies. These tensions were dormant and controllable until the onset of the Israeli occupation. Since Oslo does not terminate the occupation, the eruption of these tensions has continued in greater force ever since Oslo and they are bound to erupt in the foreseeable future.

THESIS AND ANTITHESIS: THE UNMAKING OF THE OSLO REALITY

The following is a possible, but by no means, exclusive, sociopolitical scenario developing out of the Oslo reality. It is examined with the help of conventional definitions of social center and periphery. My main argument is that the post-Oslo reality is characterized by two disintegrative processes. The first is a growing tension between the center and the periphery to a point that seriously endangers the integrity of the Jewish nation-state and with it the embryonic Palestinian autonomy. Such a breakdown can be averted either by the adaptation of a looser political and pluralist structure, or, what is more likely, by a more dictatorial political structure. The second is the obfuscation of the hegemonic collective

identities of Israelis and Palestinians alike. Such a vagueness questions the authority of the Israeli state and the PA and can lead either
to a more multicultural structure or to a dictatorial reaction.

Unbearable Tensions between Social Center and Periphery

The social center is the place where the principal set of values,
symbols, and beliefs is formulated for the society as a whole. The
elites are an integral part of the social center and are represented in
the political center, which is the hub of the social center. The social
center is the place of birth of national ideologies and political doc-
trines that constitute the hegemonic interpretation of reality
adopted by the elites and conveyed by various means to the rest of
society. This dominant interpretation has to coexist or force itself on
counterinterpretations. The periphery-center analysis is quite conventional in terms of political sociology. Since the 1970s, sociologists
have moved away from the functional descriptive approach and
concentrated on the control mechanism exercised by the center on
the periphery and on the conflictual nature of society.[10] The interest
in the mechanism reflected the rapid changes in the powers of those
dominating the center. They seemed to control all spheres of life: occupation, information, finance, and culture. These reservoirs of
power are used to formulate identities from above for the entire collective.[11]

A political community such as a state is in a process of disintegration when the authority of the center in all these spheres is challenged. From a Gramscian perspective, it is not only the obvious
political and economic challenge that counts, but also the cultural
one. A cultural challenge questions the hegemony of the elites in
the center, whose hegemony is legitimized by a cultural alliance between center and peripheries.[12] The alliance is manifested in the
adherence of intellectuals, professionals, powerful capitalists, and
religious hierarchy to a common cultural outlook on life. If this alliance is weakened, the authority and legitimacy of the center as a
whole, or at least of the political center inside it, is seriously
eroded. Cultural tensions do not occur ex nihilo. They are related
to economic disparities and social frustrations. A certain amount of
tension is bearable. But one doubts how long a society can with-
stand a continuous struggle fed by the absence of a cultural alliance.

One of the mitigating factors in modern societies that helps to bear these tensions is the dual affiliation of elites to their professional and ideological groups. They thus bring to the social game an interpretation of reality formulated by their professional experience. This interpretation is fed not just by political, ethnic, and religious affiliation, but mainly by the particular reality in a given profession. This double affiliation assures a balance and stability when professionals are torn between affiliation to their professions and their other affiliation spheres (parties, movements, religions). Professionalism and confessionalism balance each other by adherence to rules regulating the social order.

The post-Oslo reality of Israel is a case of a country losing the balance between professional and group ideologies based on religious, ethnic, or national outlook. There is a growing gap—to the point of absolute severance—between professional groups in the elites and ideological groups in the political center. This polarization of affiliation in Israel is eroding the authority of the social order. Inflexible ideological formations such as ethnic, cultural, and religious groups are replacing vaguer professional affiliations. Each group abides by its own set of rules and its interpretation of the social order. Civil wars have broken out when such a split has taken place.[13]

These processes of disintegration of the social order were triggered by the occupation of the West Bank and the Gaza Strip. This catalytic event bred group identities based on romantic nationalism, fanatic messianism, and religious ethnicity. It began with the disassociation of the settlers' world from the social order and its rules in pre-1967 Israeli society. It continued with an accelerated pace of economic growth, based on the exploitation of cheap labor from the Occupied Territories that resulted in a deeper polarization between the haves and have-nots in Israeli society. The correlation between ethnic background and sociopolitical situation strengthened group identities based on class and ethnic consciousness. This was particularly evident in the case of North African Jews. The occupation also strengthened Palestinian identity among Israeli Arabs and sharpened the alienation felt by secular Jews from any common good (in the Republican sense) that could be shared with the ultra-orthodox, Sephardic Jews, Palestinians, and settlers. Additionally, but not as a direct consequence of the occupation, three other groups developed a group identity—adding their weight to the difficult situation. They are the Jews and non-Jews who emigrated from the disintegrating Soviet Union, the Ethiopian Jews and non-Jews who emigrated to Israel, and the foreign workers. These groups fitted well into the disintegrating structure of what was once a more cohesive social and political unit.

In the past, Zionism often meant that there is a supraidentity that cancels all other identities, which leaves room for a normal dialectical relationship between professional groups caring for themselves, but also for the society as a whole. Zionism also meant providing the cultural bases on which the alliance between the center and periphery would be constructed. The fragmentation of this supraidentity into subidentities reveals the collapse of Zionism as a hegemonizing culture.[14] These subidentities are at times counter-identities or just complementary ones. More important, they dominate and regulate collective and individual conduct within the center, particularly the political center, and vis-à-vis the center in the peripheries. These counteridentities may find expression in political parties and may be partly satisfied with a role in the political center, but such is not enough. Power in the political center, when not complemented by power in the social center as a whole, indicates an inability to influence the country's orientation, its distribution of resources beyond the here and now. The professional elites are inaccessible for those groups of subidentities. They obtain representation in the political center, but are unable to enter it as representatives of the professional and civil elites. Many of these groups have learned from history that only total control can bring the coveted change in their situation as a group. Thus, you need more than just representation in the political center. This representation is limited and has no real impact on the continued formulation of the state according to a cultural outlook alien to yours. The alien cultural structure is the Zionist one based on Jewish Ashkenazi dominance that does not allow for different interpretations of Judaism such as those emanating from other ethnic, national, or cultural backgrounds.

The Obfuscation of Collective Identities

In Israel, the conflict between the center and the periphery, in and within the center itself between political and professional elites, is a reflection of the inability of Israelis to find appropriate definitions for the national collective. The political structure of the state of Israel was formulated before the collective was defined. A similar predicament characterizes Palestinian autonomy. The vagueness of the collective identity is a direct result of thirty years of occupation. This vagueness produces unbearable tensions between the organizational structure of the state and the social structure. It seems that the present state-autonomy structure imposed on the Palestinian social fabric by Israel in the area between the Jordan River and the Mediterranean is not elastic enough to absorb this tension.

Collective identity can be achieved by territorial integrity of a society.[15] Territorial definitions are a factor that is constantly changing in the lives of both societies at such a rapid pace that historians find it difficult to chart the fluctuating borders of Israel/Palestine. When the territorial collective is unstable, the center's authority weakens. The Israeli settlements seemingly extend the state's territory beyond its borders; in addition, the Palestinians in Israel have a complicated relationship with those of the West Bank and the Gaza Strip. These facts challenge the border formation, as does the ambivalent civil status of the Palestinians in East Jerusalem. The absurd divisions of Palestinian areas into A, B, and C categories, each defining the level of Palestinian autonomy vis-à-vis Israeli authority, only accentuates the argument that there is no room for collective identity based on territorial integrity.

On the Palestinian side, the vagueness of the territorial collectiveness owes much to the diffusion of Palestinians after 1948 into different geopolitical centers. There is no territorial center for a group that moved its political center from one Arab capital to another. The final movement to Gaza by Arafat and his colleagues has not been legitimized by large numbers of opposition groups who use Tunis, southern Lebanon, and Damascus as alternative centers. This situation enables different Palestinian groups, living in different geopolitical locations, to decide at any given moment whether they are or are not part of the collective. The decision is usually the result of a particular group's satisfaction or dissatisfaction with the political line pursued by the political center. When, for example, the Rejectionist fronts in Damascus exclude themselves from the territorial collective, they not only prevent the Palestinian Authority from having a say in their affairs, they also remind the PA of how limited its Pan-Palestinian authority is (that is, as long as the PLO continues to perceive itself as the sole representative of the refugee communities). This is why the PA permits, to this day, a semblance of representation to every Palestinian organization in the world.

A collective can also be defined by citizenship. The Palestinian Authority cannot of course grant citizenship, but it includes anyone living in the area whom the Israelis do not accept as citizens. Yet, there is an inner division among these citizens. There are those working for the PA and those living under its authority. At present, the PA employs 70,000 people, 40,000 of whom are police and security personnel. The employees have citizenship status, the rest do not. The citizenship of the PA's employees depends also on Israel's goodwill, the overall relationship between Israel and the PA, and on the money flowing from the United States and the European Union. This is a particularly shaky basis for a collective identity based on citizenship. Furthermore, as long as the PLO charter is not canceled, anyone born to a Palestinian father is entitled to citizenship in a future Palestinian state. Even annulment of the charter would not diminish the strength of this Palestinian conviction.

One can argue that a collective identity based on citizenship in Israel is less vague. But in fact, it is vague enough to challenge the integrity of the state. The potential Israeli citizenship granted to every Jew in the world on the one hand, and the discrimination inflicted on about 1 million Arab citizens in Israel, renders collective identity at best unclear and at worst nonexistent. A definition of citizenship is powerful as long as it is functional; it is valid if it applies to a majority of the population in a given state. But when citizenship is divided in such a polarized manner, it turns from a constructive and common basis into a principal division in the social structure of the state.

Another possible way of a collective identity is on a national basis. The national identity at least partly corresponds to the civil one. In the Palestinian case, the present political structure is far from representing, in any reasonable respect, the collective national identity of Palestinians. The challenging peripheral groups of the Palestinians enjoy a disintegrative power since Oslo failed to attend to the problems of about half of the Palestinian community in the world. In Israel, as Jewish nationalism is defined by an affiliation to the Jewish religion, secularism, sectarianism, confessionalism, and the presence of non-Jewish communities all render any agreed definition of "Israelism" impossible.

The occupation has brought to the fore these predicaments in both Israeli and Palestinian societies. The obvious result is the mushrooming of alternative political and social centers. In Israel, such is not a new phenomenon. Horowitz and Lissak describe this process in the mandatory era,[16] however, the difference is that in that period, the alternative centers fulfilled a mediating role in keeping the society stable. The alternative centers during the occupation have no mediating role. In fact, those centers, such as the Histadrut and Solel Boneh, have almost disappeared as centers. The principal center is still the place where economic resources are being distributed, information given or concealed. But, for many Israelis, it is no longer the place where collective identity is forged, where cultural tastes and orientations are formulated. Without the ability to coerce cultural hegemony and homogeneity, there is very little hope for a democratic structure.

The institutionalization of the Jewish state was such that it left space for a dialectical relationship between professional elites but not for negotiations between different cultural or ethnic groups. Zionism, by definition, did not recognize the existence of such a multifarious reality. The cultural identity, Ashkenazi in essence, of the dominating elite corresponded to the projected national identity. The failure of this identity became evident after the occupation, but not because of it. There were social and economic processes that challenged the Zionist interpretation of reality long before 1967. In many ways, the occupation is no more than a landmark rather than a cause in the disintegration of Israeli society. But, as stated, it was a catalytic landmark at that. The disintegration began by political self-organization of peripheral groups and alternative centers. The occupation opened new meeting points for alliances between different peripheral groups, alliances not strong enough to replace the political center or even refresh it, but strong enough just to polarize it inside, or failing that, to alienate it from a growing number of groups in Israeli society.

The Palestinian Authority was structured in such a way that it could quite easily co-opt or destroy on the spot explicit alternative centers. But the vagueness of the collective identity enables strong alternative centers to operate outside the territory of the PA. As yet, however, these centers have failed to present an alternative vision that could appeal to the various groups living in the PA's territory, or could serve as a common cultural basis on which elites, professional and political, could cooperate.

To sum up, if one looks at post-Oslo through the quite conventional sociological prisms, there seems at work strong disintegrative trends in both societies. By preserving the occupation, the Oslo agreement and what followed accentuated the inadequacy of the political structure. The conventional means—party politics, co-optation, domination—for holding a society together seem to be futile in the face of these trends. This is a model for the disintegration of two nation-states—one existing and one in the making. It can be arrested either by loosening the political structure—quite a utopian scenario given the present balance of power—or, more likely, by tightening up the structure and making it more dictatorial. A dictatorship on both sides is a feasible option for as long as dictatorships last in an area such as the Middle East. The democratic structure, even its particular Israeli model, seems quite unfit to carry the burden of the post-Oslo, new-style occupation, and the multifarious fabric of the society living between the Jordan River and the Mediterranean.

NOTES

1. The eighteenth convention convened on April 28, 1987. The Declaration of Independence was issued on November 15, 1988, at the nineteenth convention.

2. These issues had been recognized as the basis for peace by the UN General Assembly in resolution 194(IV) adopted on December 11, 1949. See Ilan Pappe, *The Making of the Arab-Israeli Conflict, 1947–1951* (New York, 1992), 195–202.

3. These were in chronological order: the agreement on the Gaza Strip and the Jericho area signed on May 4, 1994, followed by the Agreement on the Preparatory Transfer of Powers and Responsibilities (Israel-PLO) signed on August 29, 1994. Then came Oslo B: Interim Agreement between Israel and the Palestinians signed on September 28, 1995. This agreement has seven annexes, dealing with, among other things, redeployment, Palestinian elections, economic relations, and cooperation on security matters. It has nine maps attached to it, dividing the areas of the West Bank into areas A, B, and C, according to which the level of Israeli presence under the redeployment is fixed. The last map defines the Israeli withdrawal from Hebron. This agreement was signed only on January 17, 1997, under the title *Protocol Concurring the Redeployment in Hebron*.

4. Settlement Watch Report No. 8 (in Hebrew) (Peace Now, Jerusalem, 31 July 1996).

5. The closures were usually justified due to Hamas terrorist attacks inside Israel, but not always. They were also taken as a precaution before Jewish holidays. Between Oslo in 1993, and June 1997, there were fifteen periods of closures totaling 109 days.

6. After Rabin's assassination in 1995, the peace index, which measures general support for the peace process, reached its zenith, 73.1 percent. But after a series of terrorist attacks in Israel's urban centers, it declined to 58.1 percent, which was its lowest level. It remained between 58 and 62 percent.

7. The agreement was pronounced on January 25, 1997.

8. *Haaretz,* 28 January 1996.

9. The Economic Agreement between Israel and the PLO (The Israel Chamber of Commerce, Tel Aviv, 1994).

10. Edward Shils, "Center and Periphery," in *Center and Periphery: Essays in Macrosociology,* edited by E. Shils (Chicago, 1975); Anthony Giddens, *New Rules for Sociological Method: A Positive Critique of Interpretative Sociology* (London, 1976); Robert Collins, *Conflict Sociology Towards an Explanatory Science* (New York, 1975).

11. Baruch Kimmerling, "Boundaries End Frontiers of the Israeli Control System," in *The Israeli State and Society,* edited by B. Kimmerling (New York, 1989), 237–64.

12. Antonio Gramsci, *Selections from the Prison Notes,* trans. and ed. Q. House and G. Nowell-Smith (London, 1971).

13. Michal Yaniv, "From Conflict to War: A Comparative Study of the Conditions for the Eruption of Civil Wars" (Ph.D. diss., Haifa University, 1994).

14. Benedict Anderson defines cultural homogenization as one of the principal functions of nationalism in B. Anderson, *Imagined Communities* (London, 1991), 36–46.

15. Baruch Kimmerling, "Between the Primordial and Civil Definitions of the Collective Identity: Eretz Israel or the State of Israel," in *Comparative Social Dynamics: Essay in Honor of N. S. Eisenstadt,* edited by E. Cohen, M. Lissak, and U. Almagor (Boulder, CO, 1985).

16. Dan Horowitz and Moshe Lissak, *Me-Yishuv Le-Medina: Yehudai Eretz Israel be-Tekufat Ha Mandat Ke-Khila Politit* (From Yishuv to a state: The Jews in Palestine as a political community during the Mandatory Era) (Tel Aviv, 1977).

8

Development of Identity Under the Oppression of Occupation: The Palestinian Case

Nadera Shalhoub-Kevorkian

INTRODUCTION

Samer is a four-year-old boy who lives in one of the West Bank villages. His story begins before his conception. He is the son of a family that had lost its land and property in Jaffa in 1948. Although happiness generally prevails in a family when its firstborn is a son, Samer's family was not able to experience full happiness because his father was in prison when Samer was born. Like most Palestinians, his father was imprisoned for political reasons. Samer hoped that one day he would meet his father, the one with whom he conversed through the photograph on the wall. After three years of talking to the photograph and awaiting the day of his first meeting with his father, his prayers were answered. He was very excited by his father's stories about prison and imprisonment. He talked about his father with great pride. He boasted to his friends about the power and love he received from his dad. Later on, Samer became worried because he learned that his father was looking for employment. Samer's father lost some of the patience and tolerance he had for his son because of the pressures of being unemployed. The political situation and the Intifada made things more difficult for Samer's family. Samer's father became very frustrated, and his mother took up embroidery and sewing to support the family. Being with his father all the time, Samer learned from what his father told him: "My father taught me that we are Palestinians, and I should take care of everything I have . . . my sister . . . my job . . . everything." The months passed and Samer's father was unable to find a job because of his political record. Finally he found work with relatives working in a quarry. When he received his first pay, he bought Samer a chick that became Samer's best friend. Three days later his father was arrested again; the military authorities decided to demolish his house three days afterwards. Samer was in the nursery when he learned about the demolition. He ran to his house to find the bulldozers ready to do the job for which they were called. He ran toward the house but his mother prevented him from reaching it. He began to cry, shout, and beg those around him to help him rescue the chick he left in the house. The soldiers would not hear his pleas and no one was able to help him. He cried to his grandfather that the chick was the only present he had received from his father. No one could hear his cries as they mourned the loss of their home and the imprisonment of their son. Samer never forgot the loss of his beautiful yellow chick and companion. All that remained for him was the food in his pocket for his chick, and the remnants of its odor on his hands.

The saga of Samer is only one of thousands of stories that reflect the pain and agony Palestinian children endure throughout their childhood. I am a member of a group of clinicians who worked with these children; we feel obliged to articulate their unvoiced cries, their terror that was never addressed or termed as such. In this chapter I will focus on the effects of political repression and oppression, and the long years of occupation on the building and destruction of the Palestinian child's identity.

Although the topic of identity development in children has received extensive attention by psychologists, it remains fertile ground for social scientists who wish to liberate themselves from traditional theory of child psychosocial development. There is ample conceptual, constructual, theoretical, and empirical evidence available to psychologists to predict the global course of development in children. Sociologists, political scientists, and other social scientists also have delineated many of the variables and factors that influence the course of change that takes place naturally within societies. This plethora of scientific evidence, however, was accumulated mainly by Westerners about Western societies. Unfortunately, the relatively sparse available knowledge accumulated about Asian, African, and Latin American societies, was also either gathered by Western researchers or interpreted within the context of Western theories and constructs. Native researchers in developing countries are cognizant of the fact that a substantial amount of the information, data, and artifacts collected about their societies and culture is held "in trust" in the archives and data banks of the developed nations. In essence, we argue that developed nations are far superior to developing nations not only economically, militarily, and technologically, but, far more ominously, in their knowledge about developing nations. We (developing nations) are studied, examined, and analyzed by others (developed nations) more than we study, examine, and analyze our selves. Hence, any analysis of the development of identity in transitional societies we present today is to some extent "hostage" to this epistemological "bondage." Furthermore, the expansive nature of the topic dictates that I delineate the limits of the argument prior to delving into my presentation.

First, I would like to make it clear that it is not my intention to present, argue, or expound on the natural development of identity in children. Any deserving textbook on psychosocial and child development can outperform my effort. Nor do I intend to focus on the nature of individual identity development in children. The purpose of my presentation is the analytical examination of the course of collective national identity in transitional societies. More specifically, I will focus on the manner in which the collective identity a society develops within the context of the conflict it finds itself embroiled in, that is, between the "image" it draws for itself and the "image" the other wishes to impose on it. In other words, the gist of my first argument is that the development of identity in transitional societies (developing societies) is inherently one of conflict.

Second, it is not the intention of this presentation to focus on societies undergoing natural social change. Instead, the thrust is on societies that are undergoing a transition from political liberation from colonialism (or occupation), to liberation from cultural hegemony. The struggle for liberation in these societies, I argue, has a profound effect on how the collective identity develops. Finally, for illustrative purposes, as I am most familiar with a society (Palestinian) that is in the midst of this transitional process, I will utilize my experience to shed light on the proposed arguments.

THE CONCEPT OF IDENTITY IN NON-WESTERN SOCIETIES

Although the term "identity" is the object of my discourse and analysis, I am not quite certain how alien this term is to non-Western societies, especially those in Asia and Africa. The modern

Arabic term for identity (*howiyya*) seems to be a recent phenomenon. Barghouthi (1996), for example, could not find the term mentioned in Arabic lexicons prior to the mid-nineteenth century. He cites Bustani (1819–1883) showing that the term has both philosophic and linguistic roots. Linguistically, it is derived from the singular pronoun "howa" (he) denoting "the absolute truth that enfolds all truths of the unknown just as a kernel unfolds its own potential tree" (150). Furthermore, the term could also be derived from the "union with the self"; that is, complete personal identity. Hence, the term identity in Arabic juxtaposes, derives, and unites the individual with the collective.

The diffusion between the individual and the collective also appears to be true in African societies. For example, there are no comparable terms for "uncle," "aunt," or "niece" in Xosa. No linguistic differentiation is made between father and uncle, mother and aunt, daughter and niece. Personal identity is derived from the collective one. The former unfolds only within the realm of the latter. Hence, personal identity is also derived from the historic development of the collective identity. Palestinian identity, for example, is a product of Arab, Muslim-Christian, and national legacies. Its origin, as is the case in many African and Asian societies, is tribal. Consequently, one cannot address a people's collective identity divorced from its legacy and culture. Heritage provides the adhesive that maintains the integrity of identity. The destruction of a people's culture is tantamount to the destruction of its identity.

IDENTITY DEVELOPMENT WITHIN AN OCCUPATION RELATIONSHIP

Fanon (1963) elucidated the relationship between the colonized/occupied and the colonizer/occupier as one of continued conflict. The colonizer/occupier does not relinquish his dream of subjugating the native, who, in turn, refuses to relinquish his aspiration of gaining independence from his colonizer/occupier. Physical subjugation, the occupier learns, however, cannot be maintained indefinitely and without great cost. Unfortunately, the occupier's dream of subjugating the native does not extinguish itself as one relinquishes physical control over the native. The occupier's aspiration finds its expression in the colonization of the native's culture, and ultimately, the colonization of his or her mind and identity. The native, on the other hand, tries desperately to rediscover his or her identity by navigating the pages of his or her own history and culture. The occupier, aware of this need, craftily tries to provide the native with a map whose landmarks are not etched by the native's ancestors. The quest for indigenous landmarks becomes of crucial importance. The emerging collective identity of his nation in transition thus becomes contingent on the landmarks it assimilates.

It is within this context that we postulate that the development of identity within occupied societies is inherently one of conflict. The image the colonizer/occupier desires for the native to formulate for his or her own identity is essentially that of the colonizer/occupier, but packaged in native clothing. It is this identity that Steve Biko referred to as "Whites walking in Black skin." This process can be achieved only through colonization of the mind, the culture, and the historical legacy. Identity thus becomes the battleground between national assertion on the one hand, and domination and subjugation by the occupying power on the other hand.

Children develop their identities in a series of ever increasing-decreasing and expanding-contracting concentric cultural circles. The number of circles dictates only the extent to which identity becomes constricted or global. True identity, however, is defined by the cultural images the child assimilates. One process is quantitative; the other, qualitative. Although I will touch upon the quantitative aspect of this process, my main thrust will be on the qualitative aspects. It is this aspect of identity development that becomes the target of occupational manipulation versus national will.

The term identity, as we have seen, may be a relatively nascent phenomenon in developing countries. Its coining in the mid-nineteenth century in the Arab world, however, may not have been a capricious event. The advent of the modern Arab collective identity is highly correlated with the advent of Arab nationalism during that period. Prior to that, the concentric circles encompassing Arab identity were limited to the religious (primarily Muslim) and the tribal. Palestinian identity became crystallized and strengthened in direct proportion to the strength of Palestinian nationalism. The collective identity of those inhabiting Palestine prior to World War I was primarily Muslim-Arab-tribal. Arab identity superseded Palestinian collective identity only prior to the disintegration of Palestine in 1948 and the rise of the Palestinian national resistance movement in the early sixties. Recent studies conducted by myself and other psychologists show that Palestinian national identity is a direct function of the contiguity between the Palestinian national resistance movement and the population it influences directly (Baker, 1990; Mahjoub et al., 1989).

For example, on the one hand, Palestinian children living in Palestine (the West Bank and Gaza Strip), Syria, and Lebanon identify themselves as Palestinian in word and social representation (e.g., choosing Palestinian themes and colors in free drawing). On the other hand, Palestinian children born and living in Israel do not identify themselves primarily as Palestinian in word or social representation. While Palestinian children living in Israeli occupied Palestine and Palestinian refugee camps in Syria and Lebanon identified themselves as Palestinian, Palestinian children living in Israel identified themselves as Israeli-Arabs or "Arabs of the inside." Furthermore, while the national colors of Palestine (red, green, black, and white) dominated the drawings of the former group, the national colors of Israel (blue and white) dominated the drawings of the latter group. Hence, we can detect the battle here between the assertion and repression of national identity. Although Arabs living in Israel are ethnically Palestinian, Israel adamantly resists and combats such a development by fragmenting the collective national identity of Palestinians living in Israel into subcollective identities such as Moslems, Christians, Druze, and Bedouins encapsulated within a larger and incongruent structure called Israeli-Arabs. In essence, Israeli policy reverts the collective identity of the Israelis under its rule to mid-nineteenth century levels.

The collective identity of Palestinians in Israel, Miari (1986, 1992) found, was also closely correlated with the rise of Palestinian and Arab nationalism. He shows that the identity of Palestinians who came under Israeli rule in 1948 shifted from primarily being Arab-Israeli between 1948 and 1973, to primarily Arab and Arab-Palestinian between 1973 and 1986. It is interesting to note here that this shift came following the 1973 October War between Israel on the one hand, and Egypt and Syria on the other, but did not take place following the June 1967 Arab-Israeli War. This finding is quite understandable given that Arabs in general, and Palestinian Arabs living in Israel, in particular, found it psychologically difficult to identify with the performance of the Arab armies in 1967 in comparison with their admirable performance in the 1973 October War. Recent evidence seems to suggest that a third shift took place in the identity development of Palestinians in Israel. While they identified themselves more as "Arab-Palestinian" between 1973 and 1986, they identified themselves as "Palestinian Arabs" between 1986 and 1992. This shift, it is believed, is attributable to the rise of Palestinian nationalism following the onset of the popular Palestinian uprising

(Intifada) in the Occupied Territories at the end of 1987. It is not yet known what effect the legitimacy Palestinian identity achieved internationally and from Israel following the Oslo Agreements in 1993 has had on the identity of Palestinians in Israel.

Assertion of a national identity, as we have seen, is the first step in the development of an indigenous identity. Although assertion of national indigenous identity is a necessary condition for the development of a truly native identity, it is not sufficient. The characteristics of the newly adopted identity must be indigenous. The crucial battle for dominance or liberation is fought on this front. Identity is determined by the culture that ultimately dominates.

The history of Palestinians under Israeli occupation taught us, the Palestinian clinical workers, that the aim of the Israeli military rule was not only to occupy territories, but also to destroy all authentic Palestinian characteristics. Our clinical work in the area shows that women who are considered in the Arab-Palestinian culture as the safeguards of family honor and reputation were used as a means of destroying Palestinian power and halting its attempts to proceed in the national battle. Victimizing women, using them as a way to force a male relative to release information that might incriminate others, was a popular method among Israeli interrogators. Moreover, the fear of such practices was continuously mentioned and discussed within Palestinian feminist movements.

Children were also put under tremendous stress. Methods such as school and university closures deeply affected the educational system in Palestine. Moreover, the economic situation also had grave ramifications. During closures, for example, thousands of Palestinian workers were unemployed or were not granted permission to reach their jobs in Israel. All this is added to the fact that the Israeli government did not allow Palestinians to open factories and develop their economic infrastructure in Palestinian areas. The overall hardships Palestinians underwent brought about the phenomenon of collaborators. Young children who were desperate and felt the need to search for a life free from continuous suffering were the victims of this phenomenon. Collaboration brought about anger, frustration, fear, and hopelessness in the Palestinian street. Children lived under these great stresses, observing their parents, teachers, and relatives imprisoned or killed. Children like Samer, who felt that they are losing all of what they have—even the little chick that has little meaning to adults, but that meant so much to Samer—experienced a feeling of sadness and despair.

The power of occupation aimed not only to destroy the individual in the Palestinian child, but also his/her culture, identity, and social authenticity. At the risk of sounding radical, I shall refer to this strategy as cultural genocide. I posit here that the occupier's aspiration of hegemony can only be achieved through the annihilation or denial of the indigenous culture in order to replace it with that of the occupier's culture. This is accomplished through a series of steps: Palestinians in Israel faced the worst means of destruction of the self and the identity. As a child born in Haifa, I opened my eyes and heard Jewish children calling me Dirty Arab. In school I learned all about Jewish history, but was forbidden to learn about my own history and the Palestinian people's agony. Later on, and at the university level, I was frightened to speak Arabic because I would be considered primitive and backward. Palestinians in the West Bank faced harsher experiences, children being the most affected and vulnerable to such attitudes.

It is difficult for a child to develop a deep sense of one's native history and culture if the sources he or she must rely on are considered primitive. It is this weakness that occupation takes advantage of in order to perpetuate its culture. Not only is the information we Palestinians under Israeli rule feed our minds culture-coated, the manner in which we begin to think is not native. As we become accustomed to one mode of thought, we find it difficult to be at ease with another system. In essence, insidiously and unconsciously, we become the agents of our former rulers. The native culture is described as primitive, outmoded, or simplistic. As Fanon (1963) stated, European colonists could not envisage an African as having a "culture" other than a primitive or savage one. In order for the native to achieve success, he or she must refute one's native values and practices, even dress.

In preuniversity Arab education in Israel, the books used by pupils not only do not have Palestinian role models, but portray the Israelis as more advanced and sophisticated. A Palestinian educator in Israel analyzed the curriculum taught to "Israeli-Arab" children. Not only did she find that Palestinian and Arab culture and history were completely ignored in the curriculum, but that Israeli and Jewish history were portrayed as superior. Arab names of geographic locations were replaced with Hebrew ones. Arab dishes like falafel and hummus become Israeli national dishes. Add to all this that in the occupied West Bank and Gaza Strip the display of the Palestinian flag or colors was a security offense prior to the

Oslo Agreements. Parents faced insurmountable difficulties in registering their children at birth if their names in Arabic meant liberation (*Tahreer*), holy war (*Jihad*), or Palestine (*Filistin*). It should be noted here that such names are common among Arabs. Furthermore, children were forbidden to sing national songs or recite patriotic poetry.

Irrespective of the method or practice used, the ultimate goal of occupation is either to deny, reject, or obliterate the child's indigenous heritage and culture. Depriving children of their cultural heritage leads to their psychological untethering from their native culture and to their becoming anchored to the culture of their oppressor. In other words, the identity model that the child begins to adopt is not his or her native one. Leiser (1991) has defined such practices as a form of genocide. He states:

One of the most insidious forms of genocide consists of the destruction of a people's culture by depriving it of its work of art, its literature, its language, or the land to which it is rooted. When children are separated from their parents and communities, compelled to be raised in a foreign environment where they are deprived of their culture and required to assimilate the culture of their captors—such is a form of cultural genocide.

The human story behind the occupation of the Palestinian mind and the cultural genocide associated with it has been very much overlooked. Samer's story is only one of many such stories. I shall close with an excerpt from Du Bois (1990) from *The Soul of Black Folk*, which has relevance for Samer:

So he grew and brought within his wide influence all that was best of those who walk within the Veil. They who live without knew not nor dreamed of that full power within, that mighty inspiration which the dull gauze of caste decreed that men should not know. . . . He did his work; he did it nobly and well, and yet I sorrow that here he worked alone, with so little human sympathy. . . . And herein lies the tragedy of the age: Not that men are poor,—all men know something of poverty; not that men are wicked,—who is good? Not that men are ignorant,—what is truth? Nay, but that men know so little of men.

REFERENCES

Baker, A. M. 1990. "The Psychological Status of Palestinian Children in Gaza and the West Bank." In A. M. Baker, ed., *The Status of Palestin-*

ian Children in the West Bank and Gaza Strip. Geneva: Welfare Foundation. (In Arabic)

Barghouthi, A. 1996. "Arab Folksong and Palestinian Identity." *Journal of Mediterranean Studies* 6(1):147–72.

Du Bois, W.E.B. 1990. *The Soul of Black Folk.* New York: Vantage Books Library of America Edition.

Fanon, F. 1963. *The Wretched of the Earth.* New York: Grove Press.

Hosin, A., and E. Cairns. 1984. "The Impact of Conflict on Children's Ideas about Their Country." *Journal of Psychology* 118(2):161–68.

Leiser, B. H. 1991. "Victims of Genocide." In D. Sank and D. Kaplan, eds., *To Be a Victim.* New York: Plenum Press.

Lykes, M. 1994. "Terror, Silencing and Children." *Social Science and Medicine* 38(4):543–52.

Mahjoub, A., J. P. Leyens, V. Yzerbyt, and J. P. di Giacomo. 1989. "Representation of Self-Identity and Time Perspective among Palestinian Children." *International Journal of Mental Health* 18(2):44–62.

Miari, M. 1986. "The Development of the Political Identity of Palestinians in Israel" (in Arabic). *Social Science Journal of the University of Kuwait* 14(1):215–33.

———. 1992. "The Identity of Palestinians in Israel: Is It Palestinian-Israeli?" (in Arabic). *Journal of Palestinian Studies* 10:40–60.

Poverzenovic, M. 1995. "War Experience and Ethnic Identities: Croatian Children in the Nineties." *Collegium-Anthropologicum* 19(1):29–39.

9

Postmodernism and the Oslo Agreement

Anat Matar

The Israel-Palestine peace process, usually referred to as the Oslo Agreement, is now a part of the past. On May 29, 1996, a new government was elected in Israel, and despite its superficial (and indeed, reluctant) acknowledgment of its obligation to continue the implementation of the agreement, it was clear that it has determined to do its best to bring it to its irrecoverable end. Now that the Oslo Agreement is quite dead, it seems quite irrelevant to return to the debates within the Israeli Left concerning its faults and its merits. My aim, however, in this chapter is to do precisely that. It is from the desperate perspective forced on us now that an insight, which may be easily generated, is clearly gained. And since (for me, at least) despair could never be an endorsed policy, I hope that we shall sometime soon confront a situation which would call for implementation of the moral of this debate.

In what follows, I wish to point to a striking resemblance between the arguments and criticisms voiced by several opponents of the Oslo Agreement and the dialectics used by postmodern philosophers against traditional philosophy in general, and the values of the Enlightenment in particular. In both cases, I argue, some very convincing and just arguments are blended with fallacies, resulting from a refusal to admit a very high degree of complexity of a given state of affairs. Moreover, in both cases, the alternative suggested is a deceitful radicalism, resulting in an inhumane and thoroughly pessimistic attitude that throws away the baby with the bath water.

I

Let us start by briefly delineating the core of the postmodern critique of Enlightenment thinking. Enlightenment philosophers emphasized the role of Reason in shaping our world. Instead of passively representing an independent world, man's rational powers—being at the focus of attention—were conceived as responsible not only for the way we perceive the world, but for what it really is. The strictest rational standards were thought of as employed by empirical scientists, and science was captured as the paradigm of reason, and, as the greatest achievement of mankind, the mark of progress towards Truth and Freedom alike. Philosophers were urged to unfold and systematically describe what were seen as universal and necessary forms of Rationality and Reason.

Modern times have shown this ideal picture to be extremely problematic. Science turned out to be bringing with it not only technological progress but also the most horrible by-products, and the stark belief in universal forms of rationality was gradually exposed as leading to the now widely recognized arrogance of the West. Those allegedly shared "universal" schemes of the core of rationality were unveiled as rules mostly suiting the norms of Western society, or even the narrower milieu of Enlightenment philosophers and scientists themselves. Worse still, Western values, we learned, could be easily used as a convenient tool for oppression, since those who seemed not to succumb to the strict "rational standards" could be automatically classified either as heretic or simply not-enlightened-enough, devoid of "genuine" rationality. In both cases, there was no reason to consider either such a person's views or needs seriously. Thus, the oppressive imperialist foreign policies of Western states, as well as their approach toward their own minorities, were backed by "humanistic" arguments drawn from the well of the Enlightenment.

Criticism of these and similar aspects of the Enlightenment did not wait long to appear. Covering such diverse movements as the romantics of the nineteenth century and the Marxist–Freudian Frankfort School, it was launched from several diversified perspectives, using different assumptions each time. Most of these, however, did not question the basic humanistic and universalistic values of the Enlightenment, but rather criticized the somewhat totalitarian manner in which these values took shape in the Enlightenment.

Unlike these former critiques, present-day postmodernists regard the faults of the Enlightenment as stemming directly from the general ideas of universalism, humanism, and progress. Hence, they strive to overcome the Enlightenment maladies by opposing every belief, which has had its roots in these values, from the eighteenth century to this very day. Thus, the positions held by diverse philosophers such as Kant, Hegel, Marx, Frege, Schlick, and Habermas, to name a few, are rejected as founded, ultimately, on the oppressive Enlightenment picture. In this spirit we hear Jean-François Lyotard claiming that philosophy itself is nothing but a discourse of legitimization, created by science in order to legitimate its own rules. For Lyotard, "modern" is "any science that legitimates itself with reference to a metadiscourse of this kind making an explicit appeal to some grand narrative, such as the dialectics of Spirit, the hermeneutics of meaning, the emancipation of the rational or working subject, or the creation of wealth."[1]

"Postmodern," accordingly, is defined as "incredulity towards metanarratives." Thus, postmodernism does not merely criticize the traditional metaphysical-epistemological discourse, but objects to the very idea of philosophy, the metadiscipline that tries to reflect, in general terms, on the human condition. The mere ambition to talk on behalf of humanity in general is at the root of the problem, allegedly, since it creates a fictitious, inhumane, and ahistorical subject, instead of voicing the contingent thoughts and needs of actual individuals in a mundane, ordinary, nonideal manner. The resulting picture is essentially heterogeneous, stressing differences in forms, judgments, and standards among various communities and individuals. Every judgment is relative to its specific circumstances; necessity, objectivity, and even the "good ethico-political end—universal peace,"[2] are discarded and replaced by contingent characteristics and local, pragmatic tasks. Instead of a comprehensive system, we are offered diverse descriptions, often conflicting or even contradicting one another. This in itself is not taken to be a disadvantage; since transcendent truth can no longer be a conceivable task, we must appease ourselves with our regular everyday practices, which are, as we all know, full of contradictions. In short, postmodernism aligns itself with the great skeptical traditions, doubting the coherence and legitimacy of any—be it the most modest—appeal to Reason.

It is here that philosophers who insist both on alienating themselves from postmodernist thought and from the naive solutions of the past, find their principal problem. Such philosophers take large parts of the criticism voiced against the Enlightenment attitude toward science as correct. They agree with the claim that the idea of transcendent truth, which is independent of the human perspective,

is unintelligible; they suspect that many of the attempts toward formulating universal schemes as being egocentric and problematic
from a moral point of view. Have these modern philosophers no
choice but to bite the bullet, succumb to the postmodern pro-
nouncement, and affirm that there are no genuine differences between themselves and postmodernists?

The moral I draw from Ludwig Wittgenstein—in my opinion the
greatest philosopher in our century—is that such a reaction would
be rash and overzealous. Reflecting in Wittgensteinian terms, it is
easy to expose a double-talk inherent to postmodernism. For postmodernists, despite their humble talk of ordinary practice and
everyday life, are in fact committing a well-known traditional philosophical fallacy. What may be dubbed here as "the philosophical fallacy of reduction," refers to any argument based on overlooking
complexity and reducing everything to one simple element. This
fallacy appears in many guises, not the least of which is the "either-
or" assumption: believing that only extreme positions are consistent
(and hence, legitimate philosophical options), a refutation of one extreme position is counted as a proof of the validity of its opposite.
Middle positions, which try to draw a more complicated picture, are
discarded as yielding a "slippery slope," impossible to maintain.
Thus, for example, from the criticism mounted against transcendent
absolute truth, postmodernists deduce that all truth is relative, or
that the very notion of truth is incoherent. Blinded by their argumentation, they consequently ignore the important role assigned to
truth and its acknowledgment in everyday life. The same goes for
meaning, definition, necessity, and other rejected notions. In all
these cases, the philosophical fallacy of reduction is responsible for
postmodern skepticism, for it leads, again and again, to one radical
position from the failure of its opposite. However, the facts of ordinary forms of life are, as Wittgenstein would say, "much more complex than we might expect them to be."[3]

Thus, according to my reading of Wittgenstein, it is wrong to conclude from our inability to draw a borderline between contingent
and necessary, that this very distinction itself is erroneous, or that
there is no room for rules in our everyday practices. In like fashion,
our failure to point to pieces of knowledge that are logically exempt
from doubt does not show that there is no certainty, and even if our
use of words is not everywhere circumscribed by rules, words may
still be meaningful.[4] Moreover, philosophy, although breaking
sharply with its tradition, is commended whenever it makes it pos-

sible for us to get a clear view of our own practices. It is not hard to use this Wittgensteinian insight in order to see that it is absurd to give up humanism, universalism, and progress as regulative ideas, just because the attempt to define them once and for all within fixed schemes has been exposed as spurious, or even dangerous.

Many contemporary philosophers try to engage with the downfall of the Enlightenment in the same vein. Take the example of hermeneutics, for one:

Hermeneutics seeks not so much to reject the notion of reason and its universalist pretensions as it seeks to reconstruct radically our idea of what it means to be rational. For hermeneutics, to speak of "rationality" is simply an indirect way of referring to "the essential linguisticality of all human experience," which means: the fact that "when they do desire, humans can mediate their unending differences through conversation and dialogue aiming at agreement and common understanding."[5]

Similar approaches, which abjure traditional philosophical schemes, but at the same time reject the idea that "everything is contingent," are adopted by thinkers like Habermas and Rawls. The thrust of all these new solutions to the problem caused by the downfall of the Enlightenment is the feeling that the radical postmodernist reactions are not only philosophically erroneous but also morally dangerous. They entail the disappearance of the human subject, and with it the humane and rational voice. The self-proclaimed pragmatic approach, offered by postmodernism as a replacement for the traditional metanarrative, leads to compliance with reality, since the basis on which we can formulate any demand for change is forever lost.

II

Having laid the necessary background, it is now time to move on to the other side of my analogy, and see in what way the argumentation used by radical opponents of the Oslo Agreement resembles that of the postmodern critique of the Enlightenment—in its correct as well as in its incorrect aspects. That the Oslo Agreement is far from being perfect—far, even, from being satisfactory on almost any account—is, I believe, obvious to every decent person. This is true not only of the written agreement, but—much more—on the level of its implementation. Instead of acknowledging the implications of their own creation, Rabin, Peres, and Arafat did not conceptualize the impact of a two-state solution implicit in the agreement, the historical insight that should have accompanied it, and the full consequences of mutual recognition. Moreover, it could be reasonably argued that such is not a mere coincidence, and that from the way Rabin and Peres expressed themselves, one may easily conclude that the agreement was meant as a tool enabling Israel to continue the occupation indirectly and more conveniently.

A genuine peace cannot be achieved when most of the land in the West Bank is still thought of as Israeli, when Israeli settlements keep on flourishing, and when the final stage is still conceived of as a so-called "autonomy" that would actually be dominated from the outside by Israel. No doubt—the Oslo Agreement offered no more than "a weird hybrid between autonomy and confederation, crisscrossed by Israeli roads and fences, and spotted with numerous settlements at strategic points, in a way which will perpetuate the settlements. An as-if state."[6] Thus, Tanya Reinhart and Edward Said correctly entitle these pieces of shattered "autonomy" Bantustans. Arafat, on the other hand, has built a corrupt autocratic regime, whose economy is partially built on bribes, and whose violation of human rights (e.g., torture and administrative detention) quite resembles that of the Israeli administration in the Occupied Territories. Such points of criticism, concerning not only the "theoretical" faults of the agreement but the incessant evils caused by its implementation and the enormous difficulties of daily life, are expressed in an impressive and painstaking way by Amira Hass, in her book, *Drinking the Sea at Gaza.*[7]

Yet, do all these condemnations and criticisms lead to the conclusion that there is nothing positive to say of this agreement—that it had been better had it not come to life at all, and hence, that in talking of its execution, it does not really matter whether we capture this term in the sense of "implementation" or "death penalty"? Such a judgment is the one that seems to me to resemble the postmodernist perspective.

Take the case of Meron Benbenisti, for example. If I understand his position correctly, what he has claimed over the years can be summarized in a nutshell in the following manner: leftist groups in Israel have suffered from what was characterized above as the philosophical fallacy of reduction. Such groups have taken all the faults and evils we suffer from as connected, or resulting from the ongoing occupation. As a result, they have adhered to only one slogan, Stop the Occupation (*Dy Lakibbush*)—regarding it as a miraculous potion capable of solving any problem, from the moral sphere to social and economic ones. Such a view of the Middle East conflict is shallow and distorted according to Benbenisti (and I fully agree with him about that), since it turns a blind eye to the enormous complexity of the situation. It certainly suffers from overlooking numerous inconvenient components, much harder to solve in one coup. One such neglected component, stressed again and again in Benbenisti's writings, concerns the deep irrational psychological roots of the conflict. When we focus our attention upon it, it becomes evident, according to Benbenisti, that the essence of the Middle East conflict is not political, basically; rather, it actually has a tribal, primitive nature. It is this claim that lies beneath Benbenisti's main objection to the Oslo Agreement. What makes this agreement look like a reasonable solution is a rationalization of the roots of the conflict. Only when these are captured in the standard jargon—in terms of clashes between contradictory political or economic ends, say—is a compromise that tries to meet parts of the demands of both sides conceivable at all. Benbenisti suggests, then, that we change the terms in which the conflict is primarily described—from rational to irrational ones. Instead of talking mainly of needs and compensations, we should talk openly of historical hatred and unrealistic yearnings. But such a move cannot be seen as a passive, detached, or involuntary move. In order to make it we must consciously accept its pessimistic consequences—precisely as we must, indeed, when we adopt the postmodern attitude towards rationality.

As against Benbenisti and the postmodernist, I would hold that whoever still insists on being optimistic—whoever regards rationalism as some kind of indispensable *regulative idea*—is not a naive, self-deluding spectator. Such a person understands that there are many ways in which we could describe or capture the conflict, and that some "tribal" notions may indeed be suitable. But, being fully aware that there are no objective, independent analyses of the conflict, and that every such analysis bears specific consequences, such an optimist is determined that a solution must be at hand, and therefore refuses to make Benbenisti's move. He or she therefore insists on talking of the conflict in rational terms, for only thus can one consciously and creatively force upon it a framework, which would make a solution conceivable at all.

The case of other radical opponents of the Oslo Agreement, such as Edward Said, Tanya Reinhart, and Noam Chomsky, is more difficult for me to handle, since I find the premise of their arguments basically correct in general. It is their conclusion that seems to me unbearable. When Reinhart says that whoever thinks of the Oslo Agreement and its implementation as bringing about the "enlightened era" lives in a virtual reality (Yediot Ahronot, 8 June 1994), she may well be right. But from this it should not follow, automatically, that such an agreement should not have been conceived of at all, and that Israel's reign in the Occupied Territories has just entered a new and dangerous stage (*Haaretz*, 27 May 1994).[8] Only an "either-or" rhetoric may account for such a conclusion.

Such categorical objections to the Oslo Agreement mainly ignore one result, which had been already achieved, and then lost after the 1996 elections: the fact that Palestinian life was, during that period, far less horrible than before. As with the postmodern critique, it is the last step, the merciless insistence on some kind of fallacious purity, an "all-or-nothing" approach, which brings with it the inhumane result. It is this step which turns a blind eye to the fact that Palestinians in Gaza can (even now) send their kids to buy some milk for their little brothers without getting killed on the way—as happened to eleven-year-old Dana Abu-Tuyur on December 19, 1992. Precisely like the postmodernists, these opponents tend to do away with the real subject, and forget the importance of *normality,*[9] and its crucial role in creating a place from which it would be possible to think of progressing further.

It is surprising, for example, that linguistic universalists such as Chomsky and Reinhart overlooked the importance of the Oslo Agreement in establishing, for the first time, some kind of dialogue. Indeed, this dialogue was far from being perfect; it was certainly asymmetrical, done on unequal terms, but, it still existed! Similarly, it is amazing that a sensitive cultural critic such as Said has not noticed that since the Oslo Agreement, people in Israel have been exposed, slowly and gradually indeed, to alternative—Israeli and Palestinian—representations of the Palestinian cause. Unfortunately, we can now assess these past achievements, having lost them so quickly. We may now compare the hope that accompanied most of us to the present situation, where only despair prevails. One may say that the real fault with the Oslo Agreement is that its demise brings in its wake something worse. Gershon Baskin describes this mood accurately, I think:

Today, hundreds of thousands of Israelis and Palestinians feel nothing but despair. We have lost our hope. We have buried our dreams of peace together with our sons and daughters. Our tears and pain weigh heavily on us all—Israelis and Palestinians alike. Our tragedy crosses the borders between us. Instead of becoming partners in peace we have become partners in suffering.[10]

Said is certainly right in asserting that "the peace process must be demystified and spoken about truthfully and plainly."[11] However, not only those who uncritically applaud Oslo must consider demystification. It must be brought about also by its categorical opponents, who, on the basis of purist ideals, refuse to see that very little progress had been achieved, and the fact that the agreement is now quite dead and buried is catastrophic.

NOTES

1. Jean-François Lyotard, *The Post-Modern Condition: A Report on Knowledge,* trans. G. Bennington and B. Massumi (Minneapolis: University of Minnesota Press, 1984), xxiii.

2. Ibid.

3. Ludwig Wittgenstein, *The Blue and Brown Books* (Oxford: Blackwell, 1958), 92.

4. A typical example:

For how is the concept of a game bounded? What still counts as a game and what no longer does? Can you give the boundary? No . . . But then the use of the word is unregulated . . .—It is not everywhere circumscribed by rules; but no more are there any rules for how high one throws the ball in tennis, or how hard; yet tennis is a game for all that and has rules too.

Ludwig Wittgenstein, *Philosophical Investigations,* trans. G.E.M. Anscombe (Oxford: Blackwell, 1958), no. 68.

5. G. B. Madison, *The Hermeneutics of Postmodernism* (Indianapolis: Indiana University Press, 1988), 51.

6. David Grossman, an article in *Haaretz,* 4 April 1995.

7. Amira Hass, *Drinking the Sea at Gaza* (in Hebrew) (Tel Aviv: The New Library, 1996).

8. Both articles appear in A Collection of Articles on the Oslo Agreement: June 1993–July 1995 (in Hebrew: *Shalom, Shalom ve 'ein Shalom*).

9. Such is beautifully described by Hass, *Drinking the Sea at Gaza,* 27f.

10. Gershon Baskin, "Oslo Is Dead, Let Hope Live On," circulated in electronic mail, September 7, 1997.

11. Edward W. Said, *Peace and Its Discontents* (New York: Vintage Books, 1996), 163.

10

The Politics of Health Care in the Occupied Territories, 1967–1997

Ruchama Marton

Israel's nondevelopment of a medical infrastructure and medical services in the Occupied Territories since 1967 has served as a means for fostering the dependency of the Palestinians on Israel. Along with Palestinian economic dependency, the medical dependency created by Israel has contributed to maintaining the Israeli position of power and domination. In the aftermath of signing the Oslo Accords in September 1993, and the subsequent creation of the Palestinian Authority (PA), it is important to examine the PA's approach to the issue of health care. This approach can be shown to indicate the PA's attitude toward basic human rights and toward the welfare of those whom it governs.

The arguments I wish to present are as follows:

1. During thirty years of occupation, the Israeli governing establishment has used medicine as a means of repression, control, and blackmail toward the residents of the Occupied Territories, on both the individual and the collective levels.

2. The Oslo Accords, and the Cairo agreements of February 1994, do not seriously address the question of medicine. Essentially, the PA has continued the patterns established during the occupation, and added some new policies, which have since led to a further deterioration in the quality and quantity of health care.

In order to illuminate my interpretation of the interests that determine Israeli and Palestinian policy toward medical care, the following discussion of the politics of medicine in the Occupied

Territories is divided into two parts: the period before the Oslo Accords in 1993, and the period following these agreements.

THE PERIOD FROM 1967 TO 1993

The Establishment of Medical Dependency in the Occupied Territories

The Fourth Geneva Convention (1949) states in Article 56 that "the occupying power has the duty of ensuring and maintaining, with the cooperation of national and local authorities, the medical and hospital establishments and services . . . [as well as] public health and hygiene in the occupied territories." The occupying power is required to make health services in the Occupied Territories equal to those provided in the conquering state. Note that such an approach accords with the first proclamation that the Israeli army issued after entering the West Bank in June 1967: "The Israeli army entered into the region today and took command of insuring public order and security . . . the essential services in the region will function as usual."

Physicians for Human Rights (PHR)–Israel was founded in 1988 as a response to the Intifada. From the beginning, we at PHR chose to inquire about whether the occupying power did in fact stand by its promise to ensure the functioning of essential services for the civilian population. The first report published by PHR in 1989 was on the state of the health services in the Gaza Strip. Our basic assumption was that the Israeli Government's general approach toward the Palestinians is expressed through the specific field of health care (in its broader sense). Our report said:

In order to describe the situation of the medical services in the Gaza Strip, one must note two contrasting trends: on [the] one hand, there is advancement in the population's health conditions, which is expressed by a decline in the infant mortality rate (from 86/1000 in 1970 to 28.1/1000 in 1988); a decline in the number of cases of whooping cough among children (30.1 in 1970 in contrast to 0 in 1980). On the other hand, the tendency of stagnation must be noted, especially in the development of independent local health services. Medicine in the Gaza Strip during the entire period of the occupation has been and remains completely dependent on Israeli medicine. Modern equipment and modern medical technology in Israeli hospitals have been at the service of the Gazan residents, but they were not given the chance to develop high-standard medicine in their own hospitals. The Gaza Strip population has no representation at the decision-making level on relevant budgetary issues, or of the development and distribution of resources—which are completely in the hands of the Civil Administration and the Israeli authorities. During the Intifada there was a steep rise in medical needs. Residents in need of medical services are completely dependent on the decisions of the military government and the state leadership and the giving of these services is tied to political, not medical/professional policy.

What does this information mean? First, it demonstrates that in one area of importance to the state of Israel, the immunization of infants, there was significant improvement. The main reason for this improvement was probably based on Israel's fear that contagious children's diseases might spread from the Gaza Strip to Israel. The success of the immunization campaign contributed significantly to the reduction in infant mortality. The infant mortality rate in Gaza, however, is still three to four times higher than in the state of Israel, which is directly related to overall deficiencies in the infrastructure and medical services in the Gaza Strip. A proper sewage system has never been installed in Gaza, and an open sewer flows freely in the streets, increasing the prevalence of infectious disease among infants and children. The risk of infectious disease is high, as infants and children (especially girls) do not receive adequate nutrition. Anemia, for example, is a common health problem caused by substandard nutrition, which often leads to susceptibility toward other diseases.

Second, our report showed that Palestinians were prevented from participating in the decision-making process concerning their own health. The health budget for the Gaza Strip (as well as for the West Bank) was classified information, and therefore not accessible to the public. The Israeli Civil Administration for Gaza made all of the decisions, including firing doctors without reason, deciding on the employment of medical personnel and even on the number of cleaning personnel at a given hospital, and making regulations related to the acquisition and maintenance of medical equipment.

Some Results of Israel's Refusal to Invest in Health Services in the Occupied Territories

At the beginning of the occupation in 1967, Israel took over a health system in which 85 percent of the services were government financed. People in the Occupied Territories were exempt from payment for health services in government hospitals until 1974. This situation continued in the government hospitals that were run by the civil administration of the Israeli army. In 1974, a program of medical insurance was enacted by the Israeli military administration. The administration limited the provision of government medical services to only those people who became insured, and thus reduced the number of Palestinians who could use the health services. Simultaneously, during the following years, the quality of the health services was reduced and the cost of the medical insurance was increased. These health services, run by the civil administration, were financed by the Palestinian population exclusively, through a combination of taxes, insurance, and payment by the uninsured for services at hospitals and clinics. Note also that the list of services covered by medical insurance was never publicized, and a quota system for medical treatment in Israel was employed by the Israeli administration.

With the beginning of PHR's activity in 1988, we demanded from the civil administration a list of medical benefits and rights for the Palestinians who had paid for their medical insurance. Five years went by before we received a response, which was, even then, inadequate. During that time there was an attempt on the part of the civil administration to cover up the fact that no such list of benefits and rights existed.

A turning point for the worse in the quality and quantity of health services took place in the first year of the Intifada, 1988. The percentage of those insured fell from 75 percent of the population to 30 percent of the population in both the West Bank and the Gaza Strip. Most of the insured were now people who were obligated to be insured because they were employed by the civil administration, or were registered workers in Israel, so the payment for the insurance was automatically deducted from their salaries. An additional small number of welfare recipients were eligible to receive coverage for health services from the civil administration. The visible expression of the decline in health care covered by the government was the fact that in government hospitals there was an occupancy rate of only 50–60 percent, while in private hospitals there was a critical shortage of beds.

We at PHR are interested in comparing the medical services available to the citizens of Israel with those available to Palestinians in the Occupied Territories. In 1990, PHR did a survey comparing the health services in Jenin and Nablus with the municipal health services in Tel Aviv. In Nablus there were two government hospitals, Raphidia and El Watani. These two, together with the private hospitals, served the residents of Nablus, Jenin, Kalkilya, and Tul-Karem—a population of 450,000. In Israel, the municipal hospitals of Tel Aviv, Ichilov, Rokach (formerly Hadassah), and Hakirya served a similarly sized population. In comparing Tel Aviv with Nablus, the ratio of hospital beds was 4.4:1. A comparison between public hospital departments in Nablus and those in Tel Aviv shows that less than 40 percent of the units that existed in the Tel Aviv municipal hospital existed in the Nablus government hospitals (see Table 10.1).

Table 10.1
Comparison of Existing Facilities in Medical Departments at the Nablus Government Hospital and Tel Aviv Medical Center

Department	Tel Aviv Medical Center	Government Hospital Nablus
Internal	+	+
Acute Geriatrics	+	−
Neurology	+	−
Oncology	+	−
Intensive Care	+	−
Dermatology	+	−
General Surgery	+	+
Neurological Surgery	+	−
Orthopedic	+	+
Chest/Heart Surgery	+	−
Urology	+	+
Ophthalmology	+	+
Ear/Nose/Throat	+	+
Oral Surgery	+	−
Long-term Geriatrics	+	−
Rehabilitation	+	−
Pediatrics	+	+
Psychiatric	+	−
Gynecology	+	−
Obstetrics	+	+
Neonatology	+	−

Source: PHR Survey, 1990.

In the Occupied Territories the number of hospital beds per 1,000 residents in 1967 was 1.8, in 1992, it dropped to 0.6. The total number of hospital beds, 1,477, has stayed the same for twenty-five years, but the population has doubled. The number of hospital beds per 1,000 residents in 1990 was 6.1 in Israel, and 4.2 in Jordan. In 1992, government expenditures on health services per capita was $500 in Israel, and $18–23 in the Occupied Territories. A common claim made in Israel in public was that during the years of the occupation the standard of living of the Palestinians steadily improved. This claim is seen to be false, at least in the realm of health care, when one is confronted with these findings.

Certain Palestinian individuals benefited from the system by gaining access to quality health care in Israel. The problem was that medicine in the Occupied Territories remained undeveloped and dependent on Israel. The facts described prove that Israel did not maintain the existing level of services, and invested very little in Palestinian health care while discouraging investments from PLO sources.

Medicine Used as a Means of Political Control and Punishment

The use of medicine as a means of control and punishment was dramatically demonstrated in the first year of the Intifada (1988) in an order given by the Israeli minister of defense to cut the budget for hospitalization of Palestinians in Israeli medical centers by 60 percent. This subsequently reduced the number of days of Palestinian hospitalization in Israel from 2,800 per month to 800 per month. In addition, the process of attaining permits for hospitalization in Israeli institutions from the civil administration became long and tedious. Before the Intifada, there was a Palestinian medical committee, which referred patients for hospitalization and obtained final permits from the Civil Administration's Health Officer. After the beginning of the Intifada, a Financial Officer replaced the Health Officer as the person empowered to make the final decision regarding permits for hospitalization. In other words, the minister of defense, the late Yitzhak Rabin, seized the authority over medical care from the Israeli and Palestinian doctors and gave the definitive decision-making power to a nonmedical officer.

The guiding principles used by the Financial Officer were based solely on budgetary and security considerations. The term "security considerations" was and is a euphemism, which covers up the arbitrary decision-making processes of the Shabak, the Israeli General Security Service. Such decision processes include several hidden agendas when they are applied to the principles of selection for health care. These agendas were: the use of availability of health care as a method of blackmailing patients or their family members to force them to collaborate with Shabak; demanding from patients and families that they pay taxes unrelated to medicine and to the patient's situation; and finally, the use of opportunities provided by health crises to force an indirect, or "gray" means of "transferring" Palestinians from the Occupied Territories to other countries. Thus, in order to be granted an exit permit to receive medical treatment outside the Occupied Territories (and not in Israel), many Palestinian residents were coerced into signing a legal document obligating them not to return to the Occupied Territories for a period of three to five years.

One example is the experience of Haled Tuballa, in his twenties, a prisoner in Ansar 3 (Ketziot), who suffered pains in his testicles. He was diagnosed by the prison's physician as suffering from an infection and was treated accordingly. A short time after being released from prison he was diagnosed by Dr. Mamduch El Akar as suffering from testicular cancer. There is no oncology unit in the West Bank, but Dr. Mamduch managed to arrange for surgery and oncological treatment for Haled Tuballa in London. The Civil Administration made his leaving conditional on the signing of a commitment not to return to the West Bank for three years. Haled told me, "Who knows if I will live for three years—I want to return home after surgery and treatment." Haled was neither the first nor the last one to be blackmailed in this way. Only after PHR's intervention did Haled receive an unconditional permit.

Medical Dependency Used as a Means for Oppression and Abuse

I have chosen to cite two examples out of the numerous ones available on medical dependency used as a means for oppression and abuse in the Occupied Territories. The first example demonstrates the Israeli military control of hospitals and clinics in the Occupied Territories. In Shiffa Hospital in the Gaza Strip there was a military outpost on the roof of a new wing. The outpost was occupied twenty-four hours a day by armed soldiers using telescopic instruments. Every person entering and leaving the hospital was observed by the soldiers. In the event that an injured or dead person was brought to the hospital whose injury or death was caused by the use of live ammunition, rubber or plastic bullets, tear gas or the result of beating, an army contingent would arrive at the hospital. The armed platoon would enter all areas of the hospital including the emergency room and the operating room. The soldiers would behave in an extremely abusive manner toward both the patients and the medical team. Often, a patient in the operating room was removed by force before the conclusion of the operation or immediately thereafter, to be taken away for an investigation. The protests of the medical team were totally ineffective.

In addition, on different occasions, Shiffa Hospital and Makassed Hospital in Jerusalem were subjected to the firing of tear gas by Israeli soldiers inside the hospital. Clinics (including those of UNWRA) were exposed to abusive searches accompanied by the destruction of medical equipment. In several cases, private and nongovernmental organization (NGO) clinics and hospitals were closed by military orders and were unable to continue serving the population.

The situation of cancer patients in the Occupied Territories, as exemplified by the above-mentioned case of Haled Tuballa, is another example of the suffering caused by the Israeli occupation. During the years of the occupation, there was no development of diagnostic and treatment facilities for cancer. Diagnostics such as the imaging procedures of MRI and CT, and cytopathology did not exist in the Occupied Territories. People who were in need of a CT scan were referred to hospitals in Israel. A prominent Palestinian doctor revealed that with the money paid from Gaza to the Assuta Hospital in Tel Aviv for CT procedures during a six-month period, it would have been possible to buy a CT scanner for the hospital in Gaza to diagnose the people locally. But such independence did not suit Israeli policy. The Palestinians had to wait in long queues for their right to be diagnosed, to beg for entry permits into Israel, to undergo humiliation, and to be forced in many such instances to pay not only for the CT, but also income and utility taxes. I wish to emphasize that a delay of several months in the diagnosis of cancer may contribute to its progression from a stage amenable to treatment to a lethal stage. Hence, it should be stressed again that not one oncology unit was opened by Israel during the occupation in either the West Bank or the Gaza Strip.

Most radiation treatment for Palestinians were given in Tel HaShomer Medical Center. While Israelis who lived nearby received full or partial hospitalization during the radiation treatment, the Gazans had to crowd into a van that began its journey to pick up the patients at 5:30 A.M. The van arrived at Tel HaShomer at 8:00 A.M., at best. The patients were given radiation treatment and in the evening left to return to Gaza. Suffering from nausea, vomiting, and an overall feeling of illness, they arrived in Gaza at night. In addition, for these patients, every closure or curfew brought with it a threat of interruption of their series of treatments. These examples reveal the abusive nature of the medical dependency of the Palestinians on Israel.

THE PERIOD FOLLOWING THE OSLO ACCORDS, FROM 1993 TO 1997

Israeli and Palestinian peace negotiators who were even slightly acquainted with the health care institutions in the West Bank and Gaza Strip should have recognized that special attention had to be paid to two central areas of responsibility. First, to the immediate concern for the well-being of the individual patient until an adequate health care service has been developed in the West Bank and the Gaza Strip. The Israeli and Palestinian authorities should have taken into account the Palestinian dependency upon Israeli medical services, and ensured the referral of patients who could not be treated in Palestinian hospitals to medical institutions capable of treating them. Second, the negotiations should have laid the groundwork for Israeli and Palestinian cooperation in the development of an independent Palestinian medical infrastructure.

Surprisingly, neither of these areas of responsibility was adequately addressed in the Interim Agreement, which was signed in October 1995. In the Article dealing with health, it is stipulated that Palestinians will assume responsibility for the vaccination of its population, and that they will also vouch for the cost of all treatment of Palestinian patients in Israeli medical institutions. For their part, the Israelis will assure safe passage of patients in and out of the West Bank and Gaza Strip. The two sides concluded by agreeing that a joint committee should be established to facilitate coordination and cooperation on health and medical issues. Three pages, out of the 400-page agreement, were dedicated to the health of the population.

The infrastructure of the health system was not mentioned in the agreement. Only later did the Palestinian Ministry of Health and the World Bank Education and Health Rehabilitation Project assess the situation and determine that in order to develop a sustainable strategy which will transform the health care system into effective institutions, the health sector needed $48.8 million ($21.8 million in the Gaza Strip and $27 million in the West Bank). Such, of course, did not include the estimated recurring costs of $66.2 million per year (at the 1995 rate). The actual health expenditure for 1996 was much higher: $107 million for running-costs, while actual health revenue, that is, health insurance premiums was a mere $44 million. This incurred a deficit of over $62 million. It is important to note that in 1996 alone almost $15 million, 14 percent of the expenditure, was paid to Israeli hospitals for treatment of Palestinian patients who could not be treated in local facilities.

Already in 1994, PHR formulated an eleven-point proposal that anticipated some of the problems that would occur once the health institutions were transferred to the Palestinian Authority (PA). "Permission to enter Israel," PHR wrote, "should be granted to patients on the basis of a recommendation of the Palestinian Ministry of Health, without need of permit of any sort from Israeli authorities, including the Shabak, the General Security Service." Despite PHR's warnings, the bureaucratic red tape and closures have had fatal consequences for Palestinian patients. Gideon Levy of the newspaper *Haaretz*, reports that during March and the first weeks of April 1996, at least nine patients, five of them children, died because they were unable to obtain medial treatment in Israel during the closure.

In its eleven-point proposal, PHR also wrote that "Israel should supply permits to allow the regular passage of West Bank and Gaza Strip residents who are members of the medical staff working in medical institutions in East Jerusalem." This proposal took into consideration that the largest and most modern Palestinian medical institutions are located in East Jerusalem, including Makassed, Augusta Victoria, and St. John's ophthalmic hospitals. Some 60 percent of the employees of these institutions (1,000 workers in all), which provide care for the population of the West Bank and Gaza Strip, are not residents of East Jerusalem and need entry permits in order to reach the hospital. As of August 1997, no policy had been established to ensure the free movement of medical personnel at all times, and it is still common that the operation of these hospitals is often hindered due to restrictions of movement of its staff.

Other proposals made by PHR were based on our claim that Israel has a responsibility for the neglected infrastructure. For instance, PHR suggested that Israel assist in the "development of an independent medical capability in the West Bank and Gaza Strip by purchasing missing equipment for diagnosis and treatment, and by developing an infrastructure via the training of staff for the operation of such equipment." This proposal, like most others, has been ignored by the Israeli government, and the PA has not insisted on it being attended to and carried out.

As time goes by, conditions in the Gaza Strip and West Bank worsen. In an El-Quds newspaper interview on December 29, 1996, the Palestinian minister of health, Dr. Riad Za'anun, asserted that all referrals of Palestinian patients to Israeli hospitals had been stopped. Patients, he said, would now be referred to hospitals in Amman and Cairo, since in these medical centers the cost of medical treatment is on average 70 percent less than the rate charged at Israeli hospitals. Such budget considerations directly affect patients. Imagine, for example, traveling twelve hours on a bus from Gaza to Cairo in order to receive radiation treatment; imagine the return trip after the treatment. Israel's nonchalant attitude toward the Palestinian health crisis indicates that it pays no heed to the historical context of the occupation and to its consequent responsibilities—as if the past is not sedimented in the present.

In June 1995, a year after the transfer of the health institutions to the Palestinian Authority, fifteen children from Gaza were dying from heart defects. PHR wrote:

Surgery can save their lives, but nowhere in the Gaza Strip is there a single pediatric cardiologist capable of handling these cases; nor is there a scanner or catheterization room. The only echocardiology machine available is so outdated that its kind has not been used in Israel for over 20 years. An operation that can save these children's lives cost $12,000 in Israel, the cost of a similar operation in Cairo is $3,000, but even this sum is too great for the Palestinian Ministry of Health. . . . How did Gaza reach a state in which only five out of 300 infants born annually with heart defects are operated upon?

Since September 1993, when the Oslo peace agreement was signed, 50 percent of the clinics run by Palestinian NGOs were closed as a result of the policies of the Palestinian Authority. The Palestinian Authority put pressure on contributors to transfer their contributions from medical NGOs to the Authority itself. Thus, the

PA has been more successful in closing down the health services run by the NGOs than the Israeli administration had been. Another factor contributing to the decline in NGO activities is that the Oslo Accords created in some of the contributors such an unrealistic feeling that peace has been achieved, that they have transferred their contributions to other regions in the world, such as Bosnia and Rwanda. The closure of the NGO clinics plus the reduction in contributions to the PA caused an estimated cut of more than 20 percent in Palestinian health services in comparison with those that existed before the Oslo Accords.

The PA receives contributions from the European Union (EU) and other sources for the development of medical services, but does not publish data on the size of the contributions or the purposes for which they were used; nor does it publish data on the cost of the medical services and medical equipment that were bought with the contributions. In addition to the PA's attempt at centralization and control, private economic interests also have a damaging influence on the health policy. This is illustrated by the story of the CT scanner in the Gaza Strip. In February 1994, during the trilateral conference (Egypt, Palestine, and Israel) about the future of the Palestinian health system, I spoke about the lack of a CT unit in Gaza. The director of the Assuta Hospital in Tel Aviv decided at that point to contribute a used CT scanner from his hospital. The Palestinian ministry of health avoided accepting the gift several times, each time with a different excuse. A year later, the CT was still in storage, and the minister of health, Dr. Za'anun, told me at a conference in Jerusalem that there is now a new CT instrument in Gaza and that another one was on the way, therefore obviating the need for a used one. The new CT scanner, however, is privately owned, and is used on the basis of payment per service. At this time, the public health service of Gaza still does not have a CT unit of its own. This story sheds light on the difficult and painful question of whether the PA is genuinely interested in an independent and adequate public health service.

The situation following the Oslo Accords can be summarized thus:

1. There has been further deterioration in the quality and quantity of the health service in Gaza and the West Bank.

2. Health is not seen as a human right, and there is no commitment to equality in the delivery of services. Two health systems exist: one for the rich and well-connected and another for the poor.

3. Israeli suppliers and favored Palestinian monopolists are making financial profits on medicines, medical equipment, and supplies; Israel does not allow the requisition of medical services and supplies at lower cost from other sources.

4. There has not been a serious attempt to plan or develop an infrastructure for the delivery of health services by the Palestinian Authority (PA).

5. The PA does not make public the size and use of foreign contributions targeted for health care.

6. Most recently, Palestinian independence is manifested by not referring patients to Israeli hospitals, except for a small number of Palestinians belonging to the elite. The PA stopped complaining about the difficulties in getting exit permits for patients ("We do not need your favors"). This policy relieves the PA from pressure by its citizens to receive referrals for treatments in Israel.

7. The PA policy of centralization has entailed closing down nongovernmental organization (NGO) care facilities.

8. Israel continues treating the Palestinians as an occupied people, and does not fulfill even the minimal agreements dealing with health care: safe passage for patients and medical professionals between the Gaza Strip, the West Bank, and East Jerusalem is not granted. Such is especially critical during periods of closure and curfews. Israel has also failed to grant the free passage of medicines, medical equipment, and supplies.

Plato said over two thousand years ago that the ability to sustain oneself physically is a necessary condition for realizing political freedom. People living without a guarantee of basic health care are therefore handicapped in their participation in the development of their society. As with the basic rights of security from menace and from starvation, health care is increasingly seen as a basic human right, which must be provided by governments. The idleness of both the state of Israel and the PA, with regard to developing health services for Palestinians, expresses an underlying similarity between Israel and the PA. Each side, for its own reasons, ignores the multiple deficiencies in the present health system, and attempts to profit monetarily from them. Both sides channel most of their efforts and money to their various security forces and fail to take into account, or try to satisfy, the basic needs of those whom they govern.

On September 13, 1993, the day on which the Oslo agreement was signed in Washington, DC, I was in Gaza. I traveled in a Gazan taxi and asked the driver what he thought would happen now. He answered, "The *Rais* [leader] will take care of our children's education, will build sewers and roads in the city, and the main thing is that he will give us good medicine in Gaza." The driver didn't speak about stamps or a flag or the number of guards and mirrors to be placed at the border-crossing stations—those subjects that took up most of the 400 pages of the Oslo Accords. The driver didn't know that in the Oslo agreements itself very little was written about health, and nothing was offered. I wonder what that driver would say today.

Part III

Developments
Within Israel

11

The June 1967 War and Its Influence on the Political Culture in Israel

Moshe Zuckermann

The victory in the June 1967 War yielded a grave (if hardly foreseen) turning point in Israeli self-conception: the status of the territories occupied during the war changed gradually from a profane war achievement—perceived as a temporary political bargaining chip—into an object of ideological desire. This transformation was rather paradoxical, as it was completed precisely after the cheering triumphalism following the June 1967 War had finally evaporated in the consequences of the 1973 Yom Kippur War. I would like to stress one significant moment in this context. The ideological dimension of this transformation turned very soon into a religious prop of the new military-political reality, furnishing the act of military violence and its consequences with a theological legitimization: the occupation of the territories, especially those of the West Bank, was interpreted as a beginning of the messianic redemption of the Jewish people. This redemption had been longingly awaited for over thousands of years, and it was highlighted by the final return of the people of Israel to the Promised Land, homeland of their ancestors.

The fact that specific economic interests, especially the exploitation of a cheap Palestinian labor force, played an important role here, should not blind us to the fact that the religious underpinning of the occupation did function. This religious dimension was not only an (objective) ideological legitimization of the oppression, but was (subjectively) experienced as a deep religious emotion—an emotion, however, which was instrumentalized soon enough as a major ideological component in the general policy of the state.

Since the mid-1970s, the attitudes toward the occupation in Israel have been characterized by a process of gradually increasing polarization. In opposition to the religious fundamentalism of groups of action-inclined fanatics, there developed the first tiny core of what grew to be the Israeli peace movement. This political scenario should not be misconceived, however, as a symmetrical field of force. On the contrary, Israeli settlement of the Occupied Territories, which reached its peak in the era of right-wing Likud governments after 1977, involved investments of huge economic resources and an ongoing organized expansion. This settlement of Palestinian land had started earlier, under the Labor Party rule, until 1977. Indeed, all Israeli governments perpetuated the occupation regime for economic and so-called "security" reasons, even if under different ideological conditions.

The fact that religious settlers were often praised in the terminology of classical Zionist myths—and not only by right-wing parties—as "true idealists" and "real pioneers" of Israeli society, served not only as self-affirmation for the perpetrators of oppression in the territories. It also served as a kind of tranquilizing narcotic for those who wanted to preserve occupation without holding to any impassioned ideological vision. Nevertheless, it was first and foremost the religious ideology of a Great Israel—existing also in its secular political variation—as represented by right-wing parties, which gave political life to the continuing state of occupation. Thus, those who held such views legitimized the means necessary for its perpetuation. Hence, for a long period there was no real diverging conflict within the greater part of Israeli society over the future of the Occupied Territories and the settlement movement expanding in them.

A crucial split in the consensus, which had crystallized over decades within the prevailing "The-whole-world-is-against-us" mentality, could be detected during the vehemently conducted public debate about the Lebanon war of 1982. During the big political demonstration following the massacre in Sabra and Shatila, which was perpetrated under tacit agreement of Israeli army forces, it became clear that the Israeli public was not willing anymore to blindly sanction just any decision or action taken by the government and the army. Thus, the initial rather wide support for the war changed into an ever-growing polarization of the political camps. This process of divergence, which was accelerated by the so-called "Lebanese morass," culminated, at the end of the 1980s, during the heated inner-Israeli discourse about the vigorous uprising of the Palestinian population against the Israeli occupation regime. This popular uprising gave the Israeli identity-matrix, relying on the myth of David and Goliath, its final deathblow. The Gulf War of 1991 further served to weaken the traditionally hermetic consensus behavior. While clearly serving an objective Israeli interest (the destruction of the potentially greatest military threat to Israel in the Middle East), it became apparent during the Gulf War that the ongoing state of powerlessness of the population in the face of the missile attacks on Israeli cities did not yield the homogenous ("national") reactions of required perseverance and necessary stamina. After the event, no serious discussion about the days of crisis was conducted. Rather, the partially hysterical—but then again remarkably "normal"— psycho-collective reaction was thoroughly suppressed. Hence, these strange weeks of continuous civil impotence revealed the mere fact that the consensus about this test of national steadfastness was doubtful indeed.

On this rather tersely sketched basis of gradual shift in the alleged homogenous Israeli matrix of the mental perception of national political processes, we may evaluate basic attitudes toward the so-called peace process, which has been pushed forward since 1992. Here again, we detect elements of ambiguous orientation, if not complete contradiction. While objective possibilities for a radical change in the relations between both national collectives and a gradual approach to a peaceful coexistence have been established by the Oslo agreements, it is still not clear how far the rigorous implementation of these very possibilities is not actually overshadowed by the all-too-well-known empty talk about Israel's "longing for peace." Neither is it clear whether this newly established political reality will not turn out to be a cleverly launched perpetuation of the occupation by peaceful means. Moreover, the interaction in peace negotiations of Israeli politicians with the Palestinian partners, who have been tabooed in the past as Nazis, like PLO leader Yasser Arafat, epitomizes the collapse of traditional myths like "the eternal enemy," for one of Israel's political camps. But for the other, the right-wing camp, such interaction is the final proof of derailment from the traditional just Zionistic path, if not of the general "betrayal of the Jewish people." What may be seen as a new (if still inscrutable) chance for Palestinian future self-determination, means, for most of the settlers in the West Bank, the collapse of their (however mythically ideologized) world.

The readiness for peace of the greater part of the Israeli population, in spite of the prevailing war-weary rhetoric and pompous visions of a "new Middle East," has never been really examined from this angle. If a true peace agreement, incorporating Palestinian as well as Israeli interests, presupposes the elimination of the colonization movement in the West Bank and the dismantling of existing settlements; if, moreover, one may assume that the majority of the settlers (who have joined the settlements for economic reasons) will not resist an Israeli withdrawal from the Occupied Territories too vigorously, but a firm core of ideologically fanatical hard-liners and religious fundamentalists will oppose such a retreat all the more vehemently; if, thus, one has to consider that the necessary abandonment of the settlements will most probably be carried out neither peacefully nor without violence, then it is difficult to predict the reactions of all Jewish-Israeli participants in this traumatic event. Will radical settlers be prepared to employ serious violent resistance to Israeli soldiers? Will Israeli soldiers obey commands to take violent action against settlers refusing to vacate their homes, probably even to shoot at them? Will most Israelis be able to live with the idea of a massive violent state action of "Jews against Jews"?

Thus, the two shots directed at Israel's prime minister Yitzhak Rabin on November 4, 1995 (in the course of a peace demonstration) denote two significant factors: the sudden appearance of the amount of violence immanent in Israeli political culture, and an expression of the deep divergence prevailing between the rival political camps. Consequently, Rabin's assassination revealed the hardly, if at all, bridgeable chasm within the Jewish population of Israel. Rabin was an embodiment of the mythical "Sabra," the personification of the "New Jew" created by Zionism, the soldier insisting on security, but also the political hawk who transformed into a peacemaker. He was the military hero of the "liberation of Jerusalem" who had become a paradigm of a dangerous yet promising "turning-point." The fact that such a symbolic figure was killed indicates both the extent of the tremor afflicting the Zionist myth and the rift in Jewish unity and solidarity, which, admittedly, had long since degenerated into a fetish. Indeed, Rabin's assassination threw into bold relief the latently prevailing conflictual capacity of Israeli society, as well as the horrible violence that could erupt in the future, when these conflicts might be carried out. It is not surprising, then, that immediately after the assassination, apart from expressions of deep pain and grief and a temporary sweeping accusation of the whole right-wing political camp, the religious establishment proclaimed a collective "soul searching." Much of the public discourse shifted very soon to an accusation of the Left for instrumentalizing the crime for heterogamous (political) purposes, but—most of all—to a passionate evocation of the preservation of "national unity" and the mythical traditional communal cohesion of Jews among themselves. After all, it was exactly this which was incomprehensible to the ideology of Jewish solidarity: how could a Jew raise a murderous hand against another Jew?

The shock and astonishment incorporated in this question, raised by many, are indeed ideological in essence. They actually cover contradictions and conflicts in Israeli society, which have been swept under the day-to-day political carpet since its initial establishment. It is exactly this notion of an alleged Jewish unity, nourished by Jewish history of real persecution, culminating in the Holocaust of the twentieth century, which provided Zionist ideology, over decades, with a seemingly everlasting impetus. Such became all the more prominent as the actual relations of Israel with its Arab neighbors equipped this negative "Angst" ideology with all it needed in order to maintain the consensual unity in the face of the fetishized "security problem" and the propagated omnipresence of a never-vanishing "Amalek."

In the political culture of Israel there is an additional major problem. Among the mentioned suppressed conflicts in Israeli society is a central one that pertains to a major aporia inherent in the historical Zionistic ideology: the relation between state and religion. The constitution of the state relied ab initio on the Western idea of the citizen, holding, thus, to the universal concept of formal equality, propagated by traditional liberalism. Yet, the proclamation of the state as Jewish restricted its universal matrix by introducing a particularistic ethnoreligious dimension to it. This is understandable in a way, since secular Zionism perceived itself to be the emancipation movement of the Jewish people. But the Jewish people, being scattered all over the world, had to be defined either negatively, as the collective object of non-Jewish persecution, or positively, by the only acceptable common denominator of religion. Thus, the religious dimension (alien as it was to greater parts of the Zionistic movement), became mutatis mutandis a necessary requirement of

Zionistic self-perception, and—even more important—of Israeli political culture.

Yet, since the establishment of the state of Israel, there was a tacit agreement about the actual power relations between state and religion. As long as this agreement was not violated, an agreement which included the primacy of secular law and politics over the religious realm and establishment, and the so-called status quo was actually kept, there was no threat to Zionist secular ideology. On the contrary, it even could appear to be generous enough to tolerate anti-Zionistic teachings and actions of minorities, like those of ultraorthodox Jews in the ghettos of Mea She'arim and Bnei Brak. For many decades, the common attitude of the anti-Zionistic orthodox establishment toward the state of Israel was complementary to this general Zionistic approach. For instance, for orthodox members of the Knesset, it was quite common to occupy head positions on Knesset committees dealing with religious matters and even to head the prestigious financial committee, without ever demanding to become a minister in the government. Their reasoning was that becoming a minister would have been an undue formal recognition of the Zionist state. This taboo was eventually broken, in the mid-1980s, with the appearance of the Shas party on Israel's political map. Not only did its religious leaders strive to gain real political power in the Knesset, but its voters, too, seem to have been carried away by the same orientation, transforming themselves thereby, within one decade, into a nationalistic public with pronounced political aspirations.

There is no doubt, then, that the emergence of the Shas party is a highly significant historical turning point in the relationship between secular politics and religion within the current developments of the political culture in Israel. Such is all the more true as the religious dimension, in the case of Shas, is obviously merged with other ethnic, cultural, and socioeconomic factors. Still, the question remains whether this significant shift would have been possible without other long-term evolvements. As mentioned, the religious dimension—however dressed up—was integrated into Zionistic ideology from its very beginning. Yet, I would argue that the real "moment of truth" in this respect occurred only when the religious argument stopped to act as a somehow respected lip service and became a weighty factor in shaping Israel's actual political life and culture. This evolved only as a result of the June 1967 War. It was only then that the biblical troops of the "Land of the Fathers" materialized, so to speak, and became a real property. It was only then that this property could transform itself into an object of such diverging interpretative paradigms as "Land of the Fathers," on the one hand, and "Occupied Territories," on the other. Thus, it was only then that the religious argument could become a legitimate part of the prevailing political discourse. Put otherwise, after the June 1967 War, an accepted religious element became prominent within an otherwise secular source of legitimization of the political practice. Some may regard it as a fortunate or unfortunate contingency within late Zionism; others would prefer to see it as Zionism's all-too-authentic legacy.

12

Bagatz (The High Court of Justice) versus the Geneva Convention

Leon Sheleff

The second half of the twentieth century has seen a remarkable transformation in the nature of international law; from being a peripheral branch of law, barely and reluctantly acknowledged as being "true " law, lacking effective bodies—judicial or otherwise—to implement its vague norms, possessing only a scattering of recognized and binding documents, it has taken on an increasingly dominant role in both the world community and the legal systems of the constituent states of that community.

From an institutional point of view, the creation of the United Nations in 1945, emerging out of the ruins of World War II, signified a determination to construct a world body that would avoid the ineptitude of the hapless and discredited League of Nations. From a value perspective, the International Convention on Human Rights, three years later, served as a declaratory and guiding framework of ideals.

From the 1950s onward, each decade was to witness a constant increase in the number of bodies and documents, international and regional, that expanded the range of legal powers, and reflected the growing awareness of the desirable supervision of international society. No longer can academic questions be posed as to whether or not international law exists; no longer can traditional ideas as to the sanctity of sovereignty be used to categorically ensure the hermetic defenses of the nation-state against outside criticism of violations of human rights.

Among the earliest documents reflecting this new approach to international law is the Geneva Convention, in particular the Fourth Protocol dealing with the rights of people under conditions of occupation, and describing the limitations to be placed on the occupying power in its dealings with the "protected persons" under its control. No less than the United Nations itself, and the earlier, broader International Covenant, the Geneva Convention, was a reaction to the exceptional horrors of World War II and its calamitous impact on noncombatant civilian populations. Today, it is among those international documents that have received universal approval, with all members of the United Nations having signed it; back in the 1950s, the State of Israel was amongst its early signatories. At that time, few would have thought that the covenant's major judicial involvement would be in the Supreme Court of Israel, nor that this Court would be so hesitant in applying it or so circumspect in its interpretation of its wording.

The Supreme Court of Israel is an exceptional court of law, playing an active role in carving out the normative structure of the society in a state lacking a formal constitution and bill of rights. It has been accorded this role because it serves not only as the highest court of appeal in the land, but also, and mainly, because it is a court of first resort on conflicts between state authorities and individual citizens and residents. As such, it has taken an extremely active role, going beyond legislation and drawing on desirable judicial precedents from other common-law countries, as well as the positive abstract values of both Western and Jewish heritage.

Over the years, the Court has acquired a distinctive and honored place in Israeli society, and, in a constant string of precedents, has creatively set out the parameters of civil and human rights. Its work serves as an example of how activist and humanistic justices can provide a network of protections for individuals against state power, and an assertive framework of rights even without a formal bill of rights.

The Court, however, has not been immune from criticism, and articles and short notes in legal journals keep its work under careful scrutiny. A significant percentage of recent academic criticism of the Court has focused on its work in overseeing governmental activities in the occupied West Bank and the Gaza Strip. During the three decades of Israeli military rule, approximately 1,000 cases of Palestinian petitioners have been decided in the High Court of Justice (*Bagatz*). A further unknown number of petitions have been lodged with the Court without coming to judgment, sometimes because the petition was withdrawn, more often because a satisfactory compromise was reached with the Bagatz department in the ministry of justice serving as a useful intermediary between the sides—a task that it also often performs in cases that are lodged by Israelis.

Few people could have predicted that the first initial and hesitant steps by Palestinian groups and individuals to beseech justice from the Israeli judicial system against actions taken by the military authorities would lead to such a steady stream of cases, especially since very few court decisions have been in favor of the petitioners. It is this accumulation of negative results that has sparked the increasing number of critical analyses by Israeli jurists of the work of the Court, suggesting that the Court is at fault in its overall attitude to the legal status of the Geneva Convention, in its interpretation of the Covenant, and in its factual decisions in the cases under dispute.

In several analyses in Hebrew of the Court's judgments, I have argued that the Court's widely approved judicial activism comes to a stop at the "green line"—the border that differentiates between the State of Israel and the Occupied Territories. Too often, the Court has given priority to security considerations, even when not proven, even when lacking in internal logic, and even when in conflict with the clearly articulated provisions of the Geneva Convention. Despite rigorous restrictions on what the occupying power may do in its supervisory role over the protected people, the Court has allowed deportation of Palestinian political activists, the demolition of houses, the creation of civilian settlements, and the organized transfer of Israeli citizens into these settlements. The Geneva Convention clearly bans all of these activities. Hence, the inevitable question arises as to why and how the Court has evaded applying the protective provisions of the Convention.

In general, it may be stated that the Court has shown unnecessary deference to the arguments put forward by the authorities. In this sense, the Court's jurisprudence differs little from the experience of other courts in situations of war, violence, and emergencies where courts either uncritically accept official evidence without sufficient probing of its accuracy, or even refuse to allow the case to be heard on the grounds that the activity being challenged is an act of state, or raising a political question, or lacking the necessary qualities of justiciability.

These latter reservations were resolved in the Israeli situation by virtue of the fact that the attorney general of Israel directed the legal representatives not to challenge the authority of the Court or the justiciability of the case. This concession was made while concurrently claiming that the Convention itself was not a part of Israeli law, nor were its provisions binding. The compromise position offered—and basically accepted by the Court, if somewhat reluctantly—was to determine the issues at stake in the spirit of the humanitarian provisions of the Geneva Convention. It is within this rubric that thirty years of judicial decision making, and a thousand judgments handed down, has taken place. This judicial situation will be analyzed from three perspectives: (1) the legal status of the Geneva Convention; (2) the manner in which it has been interpreted; and (3) the consequences of the judgments.

THE LEGAL STATUS OF THE GENEVA CONVENTION

The basic issue at stake is whether the Convention is part of customary international law, and therefore its provisions are declaratory of existing international law, making it binding on all countries, irrespective of whether they signed it, or whether it is only conventional international law, and therefore of constitutive force, creating new norms which are only applicable at the national level if incorporated into state law. The Israeli Supreme Court has adopted the position that the Convention is no more than constitutive, and thus not binding on the Israeli courts, even though Israel has ratified the Convention. This legal posture relies on the traditional British approach, namely, that since Parliament is the supreme sovereign body in the country, a treaty signed by the government cannot be considered automatically part of British Law. This position has been adopted as part of Israeli Law, even though most other countries, including similar parliamentary monarchies such as the Netherlands, recognize the internal legal power of signed treaties. Indeed, in some countries, these treaties are sometimes considered superior to ordinary law in the hierarchy of legal norms.

Academic legal scholars in Israel have pointed out that the Israeli approach is defective, and needs to be reconsidered in light of the changing nature of international law and the changing nature of the world community. Given the fact that international norms are no longer the monopoly of a small group of Western nations sharing common needs and interests, it seems that there can be fewer clearer indications of international norms than universally approved international conventions that have been almost unanimously ratified. These norms are certainly easier to ascertain than some vague consensus of the world community with respect to topics for which there is no convention.

Indeed, in determining the status of the Geneva Convention, there is a larger issue at stake, of great importance for international law in general—namely, the manner in which a general rule of international law may be considered to have become an integral part of customary international law, whether or not it has been specifically spelled out in a document. Thus, even without the existing conventions against genocide, torture, racial discrimination, and slavery, all of these actions would be considered prohibited. The question then is: Are the provisions that relate to protected people under military occupation of a similar nature and stature?

The bulk of Israeli legal literature inclines to the opinion that, at its promulgation, the Geneva Convention was part of customary law. But in its first decisions in the early 1970s, the Supreme Court held that the Convention was not customary, and therefore not part of Israeli Law, as long as the Knesset has not enacted it as a law in its own right. The implication of the Court's approach is that the country is bound to observe its provisions in terms of its international obligations by virtue of having appended its signature to it, but that the courts in Israel cannot enforce it. Hence, in practice, the courts will only utilize it as a guiding framework, enhanced by the willingness of the authorities to have their actions examined within the spirit of its humanitarian provisions.

It seems to me, however—even on the assumption that the Convention was not, on its promulgation, part of customary international law, or even in the 1970s still not part of international customary law—that the passage of time in and of itself, as well as various legal developments during this period, have certainly created the conditions for acknowledging the customary nature of the Convention's provisions.

In determining whether or not rules are to be considered customary, the guiding principles include the length of time, the practice of states, the values involved, and the opinions of scholars. It seems to me that all these conditions are now met. It is almost fifty years since the Convention was written—surely ample time for its effect, in terms of the values expressed, to be felt, and it is a half century since the Israeli Supreme Court held that it was not customary—certainly ample time to justify a reconsideration of its earlier decisions. Indeed, one of the key factors that should now be borne in mind is paradoxically, the unique contribution that the Israeli Supreme Court has made in entrenching the provisions of the convention by its very reliance on them—even if done only out of good will and only in respect of its humanitarian provisions. The accumulation of 1,000 cases in which reference of one form or another has been made to the Convention is a key factor in clarifying the relevance of the Convention for international law, and ultimately, of course, of its customary and therefore binding nature.

It thus seems to me that whatever the criticism that may be made of the actual decisions of the Court, the final outcome of its activities, though not intended, is to confirm the customary and binding nature of the Convention—both for Israel and for the world community, pertinent for other nations that may occupy territories not belonging to them in a future war.

INTERPRETATION

If Israeli jurisprudence can be considered in retrospect to have solidified the customary and therefore binding nature of the Geneva Convention, its actual interpretation of the contents of the Convention leaves a far less positive legacy. Despite restrictions on what an occupying power may do, it has ratified decisions to deport people and demolish houses, to set up civilian settlements and to sanction governmental policies allowing (and encouraging) Israeli citizens to live there. Some of these actions (deportation and demolition) are even accorded a special protective status in the Convention and defined as *grave* breaches of the Convention.

Other actions, such as those connected with the transfer of Israeli citizens into territories, are considered sui generis—as being incorporated into the convention not so much for the protection of the people under occupation, but as a reiteration of the basic facts of the conduct of war and its consequences. Thus, an occupying power is expected to intervene as little as possible in the daily lives of the protected people—and surely few facts can be considered more disruptive than the imposition of new settlers, citizens of the occupying power, into conquered areas. Indeed, in some of the discussions of international experts dealing with this issue, it was suggested that the prohibition of such transfers was so total and determinative, that it would be almost preferable to annex the area (even illegally!) rather than send citizens to live there. The logic behind this suggestion apparently being that under circumstances of mass set-tlement, annexation would possibly provide better protection for "protected people," as they would then presumably be granted rights of citizenship, with the opportunity for direct influence on governmental policy. Indeed, the annexation by Jordan of the West Bank in the early 1950s was probably an illegal act, but it did lead to the granting of citizenship to all the permanent residents of that territory—citizenship that Israel has recognized in its dealings with the Palestinians, as well as in applying the legal system of Jordan on the West Bank (although the present legal situation is now uncertain after the Israel-Jordan peace treaty).

In any event, if the intention of the Convention's prohibition was to avoid unnecessary conflict between the new settlers from the oc-cupying power and the protected persons living under military oc-cupation, the history of Israel's occupation serves to underlie the essential validity of this thesis. The validity emerges both in the large measure of animosity and violence engendered by the prox-imity of these two antagonist populations, and in the fact that the presence of about 150,000 people in the territories serves today as a stumbling block in the peace process.

In few issues is the vital import and impact of the Geneva Con-vention so manifest as in this issue of the settlements. For on one oc-casion, in the late 1970s, in one of its most notable and quoted cases, Elon Moreh, the Court held that the settlement was illegal and had to be dismantled. This decision was seen at the time as being a key precedent that would almost put an end to further settlements. However, in retrospect, this decision signifies almost a turning point between slow and scattered settlement beforehand, and sub-sequent large-scale and intensive settlement. The reason is that the Elon Moreh decision was based on the Hague Convention of 1907 and not the Geneva Convention. The Hague Convention allows ac-tions to be taken by the occupying authorities on the basis of mili-tary necessity. Basing its ruling on this provision (and holding that the Hague Convention was part of customary law and therefore binding), the Court found that there was no military necessity for the Elon Moreh settlement, and ordered an immediate stoppage of the preliminary work to set it up.

On the basis of this decision, the authorities subsequently took every precaution to ensure that future settlements were set up on government land in order to forestall further judicial challenges by local inhabitants intent on safeguarding their property. By the time that an Israeli nongovernmental organization (NGO), Peace Now, went to Court almost a decade later, the number of settlers had increased threefold—to 130,000—and the Court rejected the petition, not without some guarded comments about possibly even lacking jurisdiction. The upshot of the Elon Moreh decision, based as it was on the Hague Convention, was to leave a small option open to the authorities to continue with settlements as long as they could provide expert evidence as to the military need for a Jewish settlement in occupied territory, presumably for the purpose of surveillance of the local population. Such has been the specific reason given in a case, the Bet El case, a few months before the Elon Moreh judgment. In effect, the authorities outwitted the Court—in the cases following Elon Moreh, instead of arguing military necessity against Palestinian petitioners whose land had been appropriated, they would build settlements only on public land, and thus hope to avoid litigation in the case of any Palestinians adversely affected. Basically, this evasive policy was successful.

Had the Elon Moreh decision been based on the Geneva Convention (and not the Hague Convention), the issue would have revolved around the clear-cut provisions of Section 49 of the Geneva Convention, which categorically prohibits transfer of citizens and residents of the occupying power into the occupied territory, whether carried out voluntarily or forcibly. Had the Elon Moreh judgment been based on this provision, it would have led automatically to the termination of the government's settlement policy of enticing Israelis into inexpensive, subsidized, spacious housing within relatively easy traveling time to Israel's major cities in the center of the country. With the Elon Moreh decision behind them, the governmental authorities were able to plan further settlement policies in such a way as to avoid immediate litigation—whereas acceptance of the Geneva Convention would have led to a total ban on settlements (with a few, possibly minor exceptions based on the military necessity cited in the Hague Convention).

However, even when dealing with cases directly involving the humanitarian provisions of the Geneva Convention, primarily deportation and demolition, the Court has been willing, in almost all cases, to accept the government's explanation for their actions, and to painstakingly provide judicial justification for these actions. Thus, although the Geneva Convention specifically prohibits deportations, individual as well as mass, with no allowance being made for any exceptions, the Court has held that this clause must be interpreted within a historic context that is relative to it being a response to the kind of population deportations carried out during World War II—deportations of a different nature are thus permitted. The reasoning here is perhaps the most tortuous imaginable—but the Court itself paid heavily for its interpretation when it was forced into the awkward position of having to examine the legality of the deportation of over 400 members of radical Palestinian organizations to Lebanon subsequent to a terrorist kidnapping and killing of a member of Israel's security forces.

The Justices were clearly upset at having to deal with such an issue in the full glare of world mass-media coverage—and their compromise approach left no one satisfied. They allowed the deportation, but insisted on a hearing being held in the so-called safety zone of Lebanon if the deportees were to request it, which none of them did. Indeed, the lawyers for the deportees had immediately indicated their unwillingness to appear in an area which is manifestly outside of Israeli legal jurisdiction (not being part of the Occupied Territories), in addition to the physical risks involved. The essential futility of the deportation as a deterrent was proven by the fact that in the weeks immediately afterwards, there was an increase in terrorism and general violence in the territories (leading several weeks later to a total closure). Furthermore, within a year, Israel, in any case, submitted to outside pressure and agreed to the return of the deportees.

Similar critiques could be made of demolition orders. They are presented as being an action for deterrence of the Palestinian population, but they seem to be far more oriented to the need to pacify the extreme-right population in Israel, as well as the rabble who often congregate with cries of "Death to the Arabs" in the wake of, and at the site of, terrorist attacks on Israeli civilians. Empirically, it could be shown that most demonstrations by Israelis cease shortly after the demolition of a house generally belonging to the parents of the terrorist (raising the issue of collective punishment) and generally carried out shortly after the event and long before the trial (raising the issue of presumption of guilt). These cases are probably the epitome of unnecessary deference being shown by the Court to the attitude and actions of the military, especially since the consequences of demolition is probably to exacerbate tensions and inculcate feelings of revenge among the dispossessed, including younger brothers now ready for later recruitment into the ranks of terrorist groups.

THE CONSEQUENCES OF THE JUDGMENTS

There is no doubt that Israeli jurisprudence could have made a significant and positive contribution to the strengthening of the norms of international human rights by a careful scrutiny of Israel's activities in the Occupied Territories, and by a precise application of the Geneva Convention. Indeed, there are many in Israel who believe that the mere fact of the willingness of the Supreme Court to allow Palestinian petitioners into its precincts was an important and positive step, with far-reaching implications ensuring that the authorities, military and governmental, would be scrupulous and cautious in their policies and activities because of the awareness that they could at any moment be called to account in the Supreme Court. Such was undoubtedly part of the motivation in originally accepting jurisdiction (although a further factor was probably the entrenchment thereby of Israeli authority in the territories). However, while the possibility of judicial scrutiny probably had a salutary effect in curtailing some possible extreme actions by the authorities, the pattern that emerged was clearly one of deference to military needs. Such included almost automatic acceptance of facts presented to the Court (generally, as is the procedure in almost all *Bagatz* cases, in written documents without the possibility of cross-examination). In some leading cases, including the Bet El case and the deportation case, a few critical questions could well have disclosed the falsity or duplicity of governmental claims.

Admittedly, there were a few cases in which the Court indicated its displeasure at governmental responses to Palestinian petitions. One particular example is the "Gas Mask" case. This case revealed, a day before the projected start of the Gulf War in 1991, that Palestinians in the territories had not been given gas masks in anticipation of potential bombings by Iraq with biological or chemical missiles. The petitioner was a resident of Bethlehem, a mere half-hour drive from the Supreme Court in Jerusalem. The Justices clearly indicated their displeasure at this discrimination, since all Israeli citizens and residents had been supplied with such masks in an intensive campaign carried out over several weeks. The Court severely rebuked the authorities, and urged the immediate distribution of the gas masks to the Palestinians. It transpired, however, that, in any case, factually there were not sufficient masks to provide to the protected persons in the territories.

*   *   *

The kind of judicial activism and human concern shown in the "Gas Mask" case was absent from nearly all the other cases that have been heard in the past thirty years. The needs and the reasoning of the authorities are given precedence; the Court finds it easier to relate to their assessment than to the plight of the Palestinian petitioners. Security considerations are placed at a premium, but it is specifically the awareness of such factors that led to the Geneva Convention, an awareness that a population under military occupation is vulnerable, and requires special protection. The nature of that protection was spelled out clearly and consistently. Yet, in the final analysis, the Israeli Supreme Court, renowned for its activism and civil rights jurisprudence, withdrew for the most part into a sheltered and reserved stance, in contrast with its image and its underlying spirit. This is part of the tragedy of the occupation, part of the missed opportunity for the law once more to go forth from Zion. It is also part of the blemish on Israeli democracy, part of the regrets that will linger on endlessly, long after the occupation is ended.

NOTE

I have not provided footnotes for this article, as almost all of the citations—of Court judgments and academic literature—are in Hebrew. For a comprehensive expression of my ideas, and for references to other Israeli jurists, see chapters 2 and 4 of my book, *Marut Ha-Mishpat v-Mahut Ha-Mistar* (*The Rule of Law and the Nature of Politics*) (Tel Aviv: Papirus, 1996).

13

Changes in Political Positions of Israeli Leftist Parties Since the June 1967 War

Tamar Gozansky

In speaking about the June 1967 War, the Six-Day War, the late Professor Yehoshafat Harkabi noted that this war strengthened the "delusion of unreality" in Israeli society and politics.[1] As part of this delusion, religious political groups and parties concluded that they were charged with launching redemption. Unfortunately, this delusion of unreality has characterized and continues to characterize not only the right-wing parties and groups, which refuse to recognize any national rights of the Palestinian people. It has also penetrated the approaches and views of left-wing parties and groups, especially those who initiated or actively supported the decisions to start the war in June 1967. In the aftermath of that war, these leftist parties and groups initiated and actively supported the annexation of East (Arab) Jerusalem and the Golan Heights. They also supported the policies that led to mass confiscations of Arab land in the West Bank and the Gaza Strip and the establishing of Jewish settlements on that land.

Facts have a way of intruding upon and ruining delusions. Thus, it is hardly surprising that many political parties in Israel, when faced with the developments of the past thirty years, have been forced to digest facts whose existence they previously refused to recognize. Among such facts are: There exists a national entity called the Palestinian people. The PLO (Palestine Liberation Organization) is the official and recognized representative of this national entity. To reach peace with this people Israel must implement agreements reached with them, which include Israeli withdrawal from occupied territories.

Despite the enlightening force of these facts, even at the present time the Israeli political debate, including discussions in left-wing parties and groups which are those who are to the left of the Likud, suffers from a significant measure of unrealism.

THE GOALS OF THE JUNE 1967 WAR

It is important to remember that the two parties of the Zionist-Left, the Labor Party and Meretz, were, in their various past incarnations, ruling parties. They made up the government in June 1967, and conducted not only the June 1967 War, but also the military government in the territories that were occupied in that war. They ruled in Israel up to the change of government in 1977 and laid the foundations for the occupation policy. Major features of this policy were: the establishment of Jewish settlements; dispossessing Palestinians of their land; prohibiting political and public activity by Palestinians in the Occupied Territories; employing Palestinians in Israel as a cheap labor force.

However, beyond the measures that were intended to consolidate the occupation of the territories and long-term Israeli military rule, members of the ruling parties saw the June 1967 War as completing what the Israeli army was unable to do in the War of Independence in 1948–1949 to place all of the territory of mandatory Palestine under Israeli rule. The seizure in June 1967 of all Palestinian territories, the West Bank, and the Gaza Strip, was perceived by much of the leadership of the Zionist-Left as an opportunity to finally destroy the idea of establishing a Palestinian state alongside Israel, an idea contained in the resolution of the UN General Assembly of November 29, 1947. The predominant assumption of many Zionist leaders of the Left at that time was: The occupation which began in 1967 and the battles that were conducted in the following year—including systematic military attacks on refugee camps, assassinations of Palestinian leaders in and outside the territories, and the prohibition of political activity in the territories—all of these would lead to the destruction of the PLO and the emergence of an alternative Palestinian leadership that would accept Israeli domination.

Despite the above-mentioned acts of oppression, the two combined goals—the destruction of the PLO and the final negation of the Palestinians' rights to a state—were concealed from the Israeli public by means of systematic propaganda. This propaganda portrayed the political and military direction pursued by the government as an existential and security need of the State of Israel. However, an interview with Moshe Dayan, the Defense Minister during the June 1967 War, which was conducted in 1976 but was publicized in April 1997, confirms that the Labor-Mapam government did indeed conduct the war, like the military actions that preceded it, with the aim of territorial gains. Dayan stated that the goal of the military action was "To change the lines of the cease fire agreement by means of military actions."[2] Dayan testified that a delegation of kibbutz members brought pressure to bear on the government on the fourth day of the June 1967 War to occupy the Golan Heights; this pressure was due to "their greed for lands," and not for security reasons. Note that not everyone joined in the euphoria that seized Israeli society following the military victory in the June 1967 War. Among the parties that were represented in the Knesset at that time, only the Communist Party of Israel (*Rakah*) openly spoke out against the war, termed it a disaster, and demanded immediate withdrawal from all territories occupied in the course of the war. At the time, however, this critical position, which was also upheld by several additional groups and public figures, did not gain a hearing among members of the Zionist-Left ruling parties.

THE CONTRADICTIONS CREATED BY THE OCCUPATION AND THEIR REFLECTION IN THE POSITION OF THE LEFT IN ISRAEL

In the first decade following the June 1967 War, the Zionist-Left did not formulate realistic responses to the contradictions that were created by the lengthy occupation. Thus, these parties bore the responsibility for the occupation and its grave implications for the lives of both peoples; in addition, they continued to ignore the national nature of the Palestinian question. Without delving into all the details of the political developments in the thirty years since June 1967, the contradictions that were created by the occupation seem to be a major cause for the change in the positions of the Left. If the late Prime Minister Yitzhak Rabin took a politically daring step and signed the Oslo agreements; if the Labor Party, at its latest convention in May 1997, at long last resolved to recognize the Palestinians' right to a state (albeit with limited sovereignty); and if since the 1992 elections Meretz has wholeheartedly demanded the establishment of a Palestinian state—all this was caused first and foremost by the fact that the reality in the Occupied Territories and in the region proved that two of the central goals of the June 1967 War—perpetuating Israel's territorial expansion and the destruction of the PLO—were unattainable.

The massive settlement policy, which resulted in the establishment of more than 150 Israeli settlements in the Occupied Territories, and which was intended to eternalize Israeli rule in these territories, has become a major cause of hatred and opposition on the part of the Palestinians. Ultimately, this policy also weakened Israeli military control in the territories. This reality was understood by the leaderships of the Labor Party and Meretz, however, the Labor Party, for example, avoided saying openly that the settlements must be evacuated in the framework of a peace settlement.

It is now broadly accepted that the Israeli military occupation accelerated the consolidation of the Palestinian national movement on the ideological and operative levels. Resistance to the occupation, which reached its peak in the Intifada that broke out in December 1987, strengthened the realistic tendencies within the PLO; consolidated its international status; and greatly increased the support for the establishment of an independent Palestinian state. These fundamental changes in the status of the Palestinian question and in the status of the PLO, together with the impressive development of the Israeli peace and protest movements, created pressure for a change in the positions of the Zionist-Left, and led to the signing of the Oslo agreements.

THE INFLUENCE OF THE UNITED STATES

The changes in the official Israeli policy, which led to Israeli withdrawal from occupied territories, were taken under the auspices of the United States: the Camp David Accords (1978) and the Oslo Agreement (1993). These decisions were made by different Israeli governments, Likud in 1978, Labor in 1993, both of which were closely linked to U.S. policy and its regional and world strategic considerations.

United States policy in the Middle East was, and still is, marked by massive military aid to Israel and granting international support to the policy of occupation. The Jaffe Center for Strategic Studies stated in 1989: "The U.S. has always opposed a Palestinian state."[3] While the governments of Israel, for many years, placed territorial expansion and destroying the demand for establishing a Palestinian state at the top of the political agenda, U.S. administrations placed at the top of its agenda entrenching its military-strategic hold on the Middle East, as against the Soviet Union, and consolidating its control over the sources of oil in the region. In the early 1980s, after signing the Camp David Accords, Ariyeh Shalev, the military commander of the West Bank from 1974 to 1976, estimated:

The key to the question, whether or not Israel will have political freedom of movement to continue the military government, is in the hands of the United States. . . . On the level of American interests (the dependence on oil and the desire to have influence in the Arab states) a conflict of interests might develop between the United States and Israel which will be expressed with regard to the Palestinian question.[4]

It seems evident that the parties of the Zionist-Left demonstrated greater willingness to adapt themselves to the official U.S. policy. Such occurred especially after the U.S. administration reached the conclusion that the continuation of the Israeli occupation, without any modifications, endangered its interests, and therefore started negotiations with PLO leaders toward convening the Madrid conference in October 1991.

THE NEED TO ABANDON MYTHS AND CONVENTIONS

It is amazing to see how difficult it was for the Labor Party to abandon myths which it itself had created. Here are a few examples: It adhered to the plan which was called the "Jordanian option," and which rejected the establishment of an independent Palestinian state, even after King Hussein of Jordan announced that he was permanently separating his kingdom from the West Bank. Even after the Madrid conference was convened in 1991, with the participation of Palestinian figures who were identified with the PLO, the Labor Party still refused to recognize the PLO. The Rabin government did not seize the opportunity it had to evacuate the settlers from Hebron with minimal opposition on the part of the annexationist right wing. Knesset member Yosi Beilin, a senior Labor Party leader, in February 1997 signed, together with Knesset member Michael Eitan of the Likud, a political document which expressed consent to leaving the bulk of the settlements intact. And finally, the Labor Party continues to adhere to exclusive Israeli rule in all of Jerusalem, including the part that was annexed following the June 1967 War, while ignoring the fact that such a precondition will prevent a peaceful settlement with the Palestinians. Even after the Labor Party consented, in May 1997, to a formula that recognizes the Palestinians' right to a state, it continues to be opposed to that state being sovereign and independent in all aspects.

Note also that Meretz, which is considered to be left of Labor, and held its founding convention as a party in February 1997, decided to attach two reservations to its recognition of the Palestinian people's right to establish an independent state alongside Israel. The first reservation states that the Green Line (the cease-fire line from 1949 to 1967) will not be the border. Meretz's platform states that Israel would have to evacuate "most of the territories that it occupied in the Six Day War," not all of the territories. The second reservation states: "Jerusalem, the capital of Israel, will never be divided again." Needless to say, this resolution does not recognize the Palestinians' rights to a capital in Jerusalem.[5]

How deeply entrenched in the Zionist-Left is the patronizing concept, according to which in every situation—whether under occupation or in a political settlement—Israel deserves superior status, can be seen from studying the Oslo agreements themselves, the manner of their implementation under the Labor-Meretz government, and many statements in the past few years. Thus, for example, the Meretz platform proposes that the economic relations between the independent Palestinian economy and Israel be "in the form of the NAFTA agreement in North America," which is recognized in leftist circles as very much of a neocolonialist agreement.

POSITIONS FOLLOWING THE SIGNING OF THE OSLO AGREEMENT

Zeev Sternhal wrote that the Oslo agreement was "a quantum leap, surprising, smashing conventions."[6] Even if one may argue with the degree of accuracy of this definition, it can be estimated that the Oslo agreements (1993) will enter the history of the Israeli-Palestinian conflict as a breakthrough in the area of mutual recognition between Israel and the PLO, which embodies mutual recognition of national rights. After the signing of the agreement, the struggle for its implementation, in letter and spirit, began. The Labor-Meretz government, and even more so the Likud government, continued to expand the Jewish settlements in the Occupied Territories, paved circumventing roads, created delays in the implementation of the withdrawals, and did not carry out many articles of the agreements signed after the Oslo agreement. Since the negotiations on the permanent settlement, which should have begun formally in May 1996, before the elections in Israel, have been permanently delayed, numerous problems have been aggravated. These problems arose as a result of the lengthy closures imposed by Israel on the Palestinians, and also because of the division that the interim agreement created between the Palestinian towns within the West Bank, and between the Gaza Strip and the West Bank. The closures and other policies led to a continually worsening economic crisis in the Occupied Territories.

The general stance of the parties and organizations to the left of the Likud against the Netanyahu government's rejectionist policy, should not conceal their differences, some of which are essential. I have briefly described the policies of the Labor Party and Meretz. The Communist Party and its partners in the Democratic Front for Peace and Equality (Hadash), in all the years that have passed, have demonstrated great consistency in their demand for Israel's withdrawal from all of the territories that were occupied in June 1967; for establishing a Palestinian state alongside Israel; and for making East Jerusalem the capital of the Palestinian state, alongside West Jerusalem, the capital of Israel. These parties also demanded to solve the problem of the refugees in accordance with UN resolutions.[7]

There is an additional approach voiced in circles considered to be leftist that rejects the Oslo agreements, claims that they have changed nothing, and portrays them as a continuation of the Israeli occupation by other means. The adherents of this approach, who demand to halt the Oslo process, have little public support. I have outlined the weakness of the Oslo agreements, as well as the distortions that accompanied their implementation. However, turning one's back on the agreements, even when based on ideological purity, serves Netanyahu's policy. Let me be clear. Anyone who, in the name of Palestinian rights, calls for halting the Oslo process assists Prime Minister Netanyahu, who strives to end this process, and to reverse it. In the existing situation, without the full implementation of the interim agreement, including all of its articles, in letter and spirit, there is no chance that the negotiations on the permanent settlement will be based on mutual trust, mutual recognition, and hence the right to establish a Palestinian state. If Netanyahu's government does not agree to withdraw gradually in the framework of implementing the interim agreement, there is no chance that it will agree to evacuate the settlements and make the June 4, 1967, lines the borders of peace.

SUMMARY: HISTORIC FAILURE, HISTORIC RESPONSIBILITY

From a democratic viewpoint, the thirty-year Israeli occupation of Palestinian territory was marked by ignoring the Palestinian people's right to self-determination and a state. Israel conducted widespread violations of human and civil rights in the Occupied Territories, it established Jewish settlements that dispossessed the Palestinian population. Inside Israel, these evils were accompanied by what Professor Harkabi termed "the brutalization of Israeli public opinion" and the "terrible primitivism of political thinking in Israel."[8] the occupation served and still serves as a fertile breeding ground for extreme nationalist tendencies among the Jewish population, leading to attitudes that support any form of criminal violence if it is done in the name of extreme nationalism, as we came to see in the murder of Prime Minister Yitzhak Rabin.

Yet, especially when confronting a government that excels at nationalist incitement; cynical exploitation of existing fears; shallow political thinking; adventurism such as the settling of Har-Homa in East Jerusalem; the Israeli left, in its entire spectrum, bears historical responsibility. Without denying the importance of the Zionist-Left's sincere addressing of its past failures; its many missed historical opportunities to achieve a political settlement; its hesitant implementation of the Oslo agreement; the main task that stands before all parties and groups in the Israeli Left is safeguarding the historical opportunity embodied in the political process that began in Oslo. Together, the leftist parties of Israel must reach a proposal for a solution that will present a genuine, realistic way for peace and coexistence. Only thus can the leftist parties forcefully reject the positions presented by the Netanyahu government, which are entrenched in opposition to the interim agreement and may lead to war. The entire Left is required to finally break free from the delusion of unreality, from the shock of Rabin's murder, and that of the election results in 1996, and to unhesitatingly adopt and promote the political platform of two states—Israel and Palestine.

NOTES

1. Yehoshafat Harkabi, *Vision, Not Fantasy* (in Hebrew) (Jerusalem, 1982), 192.

2. Moshe Dayan, interview in *Yediot Ahronot* (in Hebrew), 27 April 1997.

3. Report by the Staff of the Jaffe Center for Strategic Studies, *Judea, Samaria and Gaza—Roads to a Peace Settlement* (in Hebrew), Tel Aviv, 1989, 106.

4. Aluf Hareven, ed., *Is There a Solution to the Palestinian Problem?* (in Hebrew) (Jerusalem, 1982), 92.

5. Meretz Platform, Tel Aviv, 1997, 8.

6. *Haaretz*, 21 March 1996.

7. Hadash Platform, Tel Aviv, 1996.

8. Harkabi, *Vision, Not Fantasy*, 223, 224.

14

Semantics and Pragmatics of Occupation

Anat Biletzki

LANGUAGE AND THE WORLD

Words and World. That is the couple that constitutes—traditionally—the question of meaning. The meaning of words, again traditionally, has been perceived as having to do with the way words "hinge on to the world." Words get their meanings by relating to the world, by pointing to objects (referring to them) and by describing those same objects (predicating something of them). And if this seems too narrow a depiction of what words do, then we—we being philosophers of language—immediately broaden that key term "object" by enriching the world, that is, by recognizing that the objects inhabiting the world are not only tables and chairs and trees and flowers, but also ideas, feelings, thoughts, emotions, and so on. By doing so, by populating the world with the abstract as well as the concrete, with the ideational as well as the material, with the internal as well as the external, we can hold on to our traditional and intuitive "theory of meaning"—that words relate to the world.

In what does that relationship consist? The old-fashioned philosophical realist held that there is a world out there which is independent of our thoughts, our will, our language. Accordingly, sentences in our language which purport to describe that self-subsistent world are true or false regardless of our use of the words. The basic term of this relationship is "representation": words represent things in the world, sentences represent states of affairs in the world, and altogether, *language* represents the *world*. Traditionally—and I venture to say naturally and intuitively—theories of meaning held to representationalism well into the twentieth century. Thus were born the fields "semantics" and "pragmatics."[1] If the world is full of things represented by words, semantics is that area of linguistic and philosophical research that investigates the meanings of words having to do with the representational relationship between the "sign" (the word) and that "signified" (the thing, the fact). Not surprisingly then, semantics focuses on questions of truth and falsity as defining the success and failure of signs to signify. Pragmatics, on the other hand, is that area of research that investigates the meanings of words as used (to represent) by their users—the language speakers (and hearers).[2] It is important to note, in this connection, that pragmatics does not necessarily deny that words represent the world. However, a pragmaticist insists that a good theory of meaning cannot ignore the user using the words to represent. A good pragmaticist inveighs against giving a good theory of how words mean—how they represent the world—without taking into account the fact that we, the users of a language, do something with these words. Not surprisingly again, pragmatics focuses on questions of use, its slogan having become, these past forty years, "meaning as use."

How can words represent—literally *represent?* Synonyms of "represent" that are relevant to our semantical discussion would be "stand for," "fill the role of," "function as," or "mirror"—synonyms that vary in their active aspect. While mirroring seems absolutely neutral, standing for is less so, filling one's role less again, and functioning as is least neutral of all. The "representor" (the sign) becomes, in the progression of synonyms, gradually more independent of the "representee" (the signified). In other words, when we think of the representor as doing something more active than merely mirroring, we give various weight to our semantical use of words. It then becomes important to note that the demand for a purely semantical discussion is old-fashioned, since we must be cognizant of the fact that words themselves do not stand for, do not fill the role of, do not function as, but rather, it is we who use them to do all of these things. And this brings us back full circle to the claim of the indispensability of pragmatics.

A short aside: It has been two hundred years since Kant taught us that the "world" can only be known via our human conceptual scheme, and one hundred years since Frege's "linguistic turn"—whence we know that the "world" can only be described via our human language. In this heyday of "language games," "discourses," and "narratives," we are all too painfully aware of the turn in the arrow of meaning which started with the world and progressed to the world. Not only do we now smile at the (obsolete?) thought that words can so naively represent the world, but we go round full circle and claim that our words "make" the world. Indeed, there are now vibrant anitrealists who claim that there is no world—or at least no objective, independent world out there independent of our language and thoughts of it. Nevertheless, and with no apologetics, I will remain, for the purposes of this discussion, anachronistically representational; that is, I will pretend that postmodernism never existed and will continue to speak of words as standing for things.

POLITICAL SEMANTICS

Words stand for things. But sometimes one word stands for many things; other times many words stand for one thing. And that is where the story of politics begins.

In thirty years of occupation, in fifty years of the State of Israel, in one hundred years of Zionism, we have been told stories, we have read newspaper articles, and we have heard radio and television reports. The words used in these media have pretended to represent the world they were reporting about, trying to adhere to traditional representationalism wherein there was an objective world out there about which the media merely "reported." It has become, however, an almost trivial fact to note that words are not neutral and therefore, "good" words are used to represent the good guys—us, while "bad" words are used to represent the bad guys, the enemy—them. Much work has been done in researching this ideological use of language in the current and local context,[3] unearthing trends and schemes in language use that are to be expected in a situation as pregnant as that of the Middle East in the past thirty years. Ran Hacohen may be quoted as formulating, paradigmatically, an overview of a complex linguistic condition, when he says that

the organizing principles of Hebrew terminology for the conflict seem to repeat, or maybe enhance, the classical motives of war propaganda: the enemy is the aggressor rejects peace, is immoral, inhuman, unjust in his actions and not legitimate; whereas we are benevolent victims who defend themselves, we yearn for peace we are moral and fair, act legitimately and justly.[4]

I do not disagree here with Hacohen; I merely want to point out that the organizing principles of any terminology, in any language, do the same. There is nothing special about Hebrew.

Illustrations of this unobjective, even when representational, use of words are numerous. In a recent visit to the October Panorama in Cairo, which is the public, official site built to commemorate and celebrate the Egyptian "victory"[5] in 1973, I was not surprised to hear it told how an "immoral enemy," "intoxicated" by its "shallow victory" in 1967, proceeded to continue its "aggression against innocent citizenry," refused to "embrace honest yearnings for peace" propounded by Sadat, and, indeed, acted in the same reproachable manner that enemies everywhere adopt. This overt use of value-laden terms armed by metaphor and figurative nuances to the point of drama and poetry, is not my point here. Indeed, it is exactly that kind of dramatic language that parades its subjectivity with nary a glance in the direction of objective reporting. Rather, I wish to focus on words that pretend to carry no value and thereby assume the function of straight reportage, pure description.[6]

Here, again, much research has been done, and in fact, Israeli media (especially the written media), is consciously self-reflective in alerting us, the readers (albeit the "intelligent" readers of the more highbrow newspapers), to the vocabulary of occupation. The data is multitudinous (and generally well-known), so I will peruse only a few terminological cases to illustrate the point.[7] During the Intifada, when children, adults, and soldiers were injured and killed, and when the age of the victims became an instrumental tool in influencing world public opinion, Israeli broadcasting and newspapers adopted a uniform terminology: Palestinian children were systematically labeled "youths" (tze'irim) or "young boys" (ne'arim)—even at the tender age of five—while Palestinian teenagers were labeled "young men" (bachurim). Young Israeli men, in turn, were "youths" (tze'irim) or even "young boys" (ne'arim), and Israeli teenagers were always children (yeladim). These descriptions, with no explicit value judgment, made Palestinians older than they were, Israelis younger than their age. The semantics of descriptive adjectives which point to age groups rather than exact ages (five, nine, fifteen) must deal with boundary conditions and fuzzy terms. When is one young, younger, or even a child? Exploiting these fuzzy boundaries while using these fluid terms is a political move well-hidden under supposed reportage.[8]

A person is either alive or dead; his route to death, however, is variable. Nevertheless, and almost invariably, when one looks over reports in the media of the deaths of Palestinians at the hands of Israelis, the verb chosen to depict those deaths is the very bland "to kill" (*la'harog*). Thus, Israeli soldiers and settlers "killed" (*hargu*) Palestinians. Indeed, the event, rather than the act itself is usually reported in the passive, where instead of Israelis killing Palestinians, the victims "were killed" (*ne'hergu*)—sometimes even with no mention of the agent of the act. It almost seems that Palestinians are thus even being accredited with the responsibility for "being killed." On the other hand, when Palestinians cause the deaths of Jews, they almost always "murder" (*rotzchim*) their victims; the verb "to murder" (*lirtzo'ach*) carrying, within its semantics, the blame, the evil, the intention, and the illegitimacy of the act a priori.

We have gone through adjectives and verbs which carry the positive and the negative, praise and blame, good and evil, within their seemingly neutral semantics; now to semantic innuendos and the "occupation" itself. The progression from Occupied Territories (*schtachim k'vushim*), to administered territories (*shtachim muchzakim*), to simply territories (*schtachim*), to Judea and Samaria (*yo'sh*), has been well-documented and has become, indeed, an explicit political issue. The choice of label for the territories is one's statement of location within the Israeli political sphere. There is, moreover, an added interest in recent reports, by Israeli media, of the meeting convened by the Assembly of the Palestinian Authority (June 1997) to discuss thirty years of "what they call" (*mashe'mechuneh al yadam*) occupation. This is a subtle use of "true" reportage with a semantic implication arising out of this exact description: the very term of occupation is thereby negated by its adjacent qualification as being an occupation only in "their" eyes.[9]

SEMANTICAL CHANGE

In September 1993, the Oslo Accords were signed and the Middle East entered a new period defined by the magic words "The Peace Process." Two caveats must be appended with all honesty to this last sentence (caveats which, not coincidentally, provide the firewood for the flames of political discourse within the Israeli Left). First, there is the question of historical pinpointing that does or does not view 1993 as the beginning of something new but rather clarifies that it is only the continuation of something (good or bad, de-

pending on one's political stance) begun in 1967, 1948, or even earlier. This is an issue for historiography and cannot be dealt with
here, save to admonish ourselves to beware of too easily announcing new historical periods. Second, and more to the point, there is
the very semantic question of the reference of that elusive term
"peace," and the ongoing discussion and argument concerning the
propriety of using that term to describe the said process. I put those
caveats aside for the moment (though I concede that they might
supply the refutation of my thesis), and accept 1993 as the point of
departure for my main claim: that the semantics of the occupation
has changed since that date. I do not claim that the change is radical; neither can I point to a myriad of data backing my few examples. My point is only that there is a change. How significant a
change? That is the question to be posed shortly.[10] First, let us examine some examples of semantical change.

Until 1993, Arabs were Arabs were Arabs. Covering the spectrum
from the extreme position held by Golda Meir pronouncing the absence of a Palestinian nation, to another extreme of that same nation
being an enemy to be "transferred," and including all the "moderate" views in between on the identity or rights of Palestinians—the
Israeli media had never, officially, referred to individuals of that nation as Palestinians. The Oslo handshakes, which involved a recognition of that "other" as one who exists and carries rights (a right, at
the least, to be recognized as existing), were followed by an explicit
semantical change in any and all reports about that Other. Whether
the reports are positive accounts (such as of enterprise, industry, negotiations) or negative statements (such as of violence or terrorism),
they are attributed to Palestinians. The very explicitness of the name
involves and recognizes the history of aspiration to recognition and
satisfaction—even if only partial—of that aspiration. Indeed, concerning the name "Palestine" one can go even further and point to
semantical change within the Israeli Left where, instead of the former "Palestinian State" (*medina Palestina'it*), one now merely says
"Palestine."[11]

Palestinians as individuals now also carry their own proper names.
Whereas in the past, dead Israelis were always people one could
identify by their names (with the usual additional information of age,
domicile, profession, marital status, etc.), Palestinians (or, for that
matter, Arabs within Israel), were unknown, anonymous, sometimes
numbered "dead" (*shlosha metim, shlosha harugim*). The recognition of
a national entity has now filtered down to an acknowledgment of the

human faces making up that entity and this is manifested clearly in reportage of Palestinian dead by name. This point, though related to the former admission of their status as Palestinians, not "just" Arabs, is distinct, resulting in a double accretion and allowing them to be both named (by proper names as individuals) and described (by an identifying adjective as Palestinians).

The issue of names and descriptions is a semantical issue in that the words chosen to represent the world are called upon to refer to that about which we are talking and to then describe that same entity loyally, with representative accuracy. The move from general sets (Arabs) to more well-defined subsets (Palestinians), or from groups (the "dead") to individuals within those groups (identified by proper names), is a symptom of such accuracy. Whether performed consciously or not, it is a move characteristic of semantical change since Oslo.

What does semantical change mean; what is its political significance (if any)? Returning to the theoretical questions of words and the world, or language and reality, we can pose the question differently by asking whether a change in semantics—in the words we use to describe the world—bespeaks a change in that world or a mere change in words. Furthermore, while investigating semantical change one may wonder about the direction of fit: is a change in reality (supposing such change were possible independent of our words) the cause of a change in our language, in our very conceptual scheme? Or is the change in our (intentional) conceptual apparatus the trigger for changes in the world? This very popular philosophical issue is beyond the time and space of this essay. Suffice to admit to this semantical change as either a symptom of, or one (of a large number) of needed triggers for political change.[12]

FROM SEMANTICS TO PRAGMATICS

And what of Pragmatics? Pragmatics is that arena of language study that investigates the relations between signs and their users, claiming that a fruitful analysis of any linguistic phenomenon must turn to the use of language. The use of language is then explicated via several theoretical routes which include as keywords the concepts of "speech acts," "intentions," "conventions," "presuppositions," and, most important for our purpose, "context."[13] The context of an utterance consists of the speaker, the audience, the time of utterance, the place of utterance, the intentions of the speaker, the (institutional or other) role of the speaker and the audience, etc. Turning to context the pragmatic analysis of utterances addresses the meaning of these utterances in a far richer manner than the merely semantical analysis that narrowed meaning to the relation between words and what they represent. That relation—between words and their referents—now gets augmented by a turn to the users of the words (that represent the world). Asking "what of Pragmatics" is then tantamount to asking, "What of the users of the words that represent the world?"

In a sense, one could say that my whole discussion has been, at base, a pragmatical discussion. Although couched in the semantical jargon of words standing for and referring to objects (people, nations, etc.) in the world, it has resolved, even if only implicitly, around the motivations and actions of the people using those words. In another sense, however, one could also say (and someone did, indeed, recently say to me), that as long as only words are involved rather than the explicit actions of living, concrete actors— users of the language—are only playing with words rather than making real peace. In other words, beyond the semantics of peace there is a dire need for a pragmatics of peace. Beyond the questions about words and what they point to we must ask about the contexts in which those words are used.

Without exhibiting undue optimism, indeed, without voicing emotions (of anything akin to optimism or pessimism),[14] but rather by clinging to language analysis, I will, in conclusion, attempt to point to a pragmatics of change, that is, to contexts or situations which belie Hacohen's words to the effect that our present use of words only serves to reaffirm the past.

Ideal languages, logical languages, formal languages are those artificial constructs which have serviced philosophers trying to formulate a language which is not touched by the whims of ordinary life. "Ordinary language" is the conceptual framework within which contexts of use make a difference in meaning. In a recent report on Arafat's whereabouts (May 1997), Israeli radio announced that the chairman would be traveling to see a soccer match between the Jordanian team and the Palestinian team. Beyond the very clear semantics (sketched above, concerning the use of "Palestinian" as a label for persons) there is something altogether new, refreshing, even a bit surrealistic in a language that is open to contexts involving Palestinian soccer teams. This is in contrast to contexts that involve the Palestinian Authority or the Palestinian Police since these can be, and often are, accused of artificiality, formalism, and official pretension. The recognition given the Authority or the police is an institutional one and, while definitely a result of the peace process, is perhaps also a part of the ongoing conflict. This cannot be said of a Palestinian soccer team that wears its identity on its sleeves, so to speak, and awakens us to the "ordinary language" of the new reality. There is nothing conflictual in the story of a Palestinian soccer team (beyond the soccer "conflict"); there is something resoundingly normal.

Of similar consequence is a television interview conducted not long ago (April 1997), by a popular Israeli interviewer (Ram Evron) with two Palestinians, Ahmed Tibi, Arafat's chief consultant and adviser on Israeli affairs, and Bassem Eid, who heads the Palestinian Center for Human Rights. That fact, in itself, is highly significant. We have grown used to witnessing a "representative" Palestinian in several television discussions and talk shows, and such scenarios, though obviously a product of the peace process, may be no more than lip service to it. Such contexts should not, however, be shrugged off even when identified as lip-service. Pragmatics teaches us to investigate the implicit intentions, motivations, and purposes of speakers in certain contexts in order to better understand their explicit words. Lip service itself is evidence of the intention to recognize another's presence (or rights) which, while not authentic or deep enough, may point to change, however small. Be that as it may, an interview with Palestinians alone that addresses a question which is at issue between factors within the Palestinian constituency, is recognition of a deeper sort, recognition of their existence as legitimate interlocutors both with us and between themselves. The homogeneous Arab gives way to a heterogeneous community made up of people, of individuals, of humans who partake in conversation among themselves and this conversation is interesting and complex enough to merit questioning by the Israeli media. But so novel, in fact, is this context that certain utterances seem ludicrous to an experienced viewer of more experienced interviewees. Thus, for example, when Tibi, at one point, says to Eid, in evident and hard-to-conceal recrimination ". . . not now Bassem . . .", one gets the express feeling that these actors in an unrehearsed play are working, like us, at ingesting new functions, new roles, new contextual frameworks. Deep pragmatical analysis of these, and similar interviews—of contexts—promises to provide us with formulations (of purposes, functions, and roles) that can further our understanding of the dialogue that must take place in the handling of peace.

Such novelty of contexts is the stuff pragmatics is made of. Put differently, it is clear that the 1993 accords have brought about an unfamiliar context within which language users are using, abusing, manipulating, and putting to advantage the fluidity of words—their variable semantics. This turn to use in context—of both old words in new contexts and even new words for those new contexts—pragmatically endows words with additional meanings. Such change in language is explicit evidence of different contexts, of a different pragmatics.

Whether it is the pragmatics of a new sort of occupation or the pragmatics of peace, that is another question.

NOTES

1. I use the terms "semantics" and "pragmatics" in their very constrained roles within the disciplines of linguistics and philosophy of language. That is to say, I ignore, for the duration of this article the more "regular" meanings of these terms as usually used: semantics as anything having to do with meaning ("That is just a semantical argument . . ."), and pragmatics as anything having to do with usefulness ("Let's be more pragmatic about it . . .").

2. Terminological credit is usually given to Charles Morris who provided the schematic definitions: Syntax treats of the relations holding among signs; semantics—the relations holding between signs and their referents; and pragmatics—the relations holding between signs and their human users. See Charles Morris, *Foundations of the Theory of Signs* (Chicago: University of Chicago Press, 1938).

3. See Uri Ben-Eliezer, *The Emergence of Israeli Militarism 1936–1956* (in Hebrew) (Tel Aviv: Dvir, 1995); Yitzhak Laor, *Narratives with No Natives* (in Hebrew) (Tel Aviv: Ha-kibutz ha-me'uchad, 1995); Uri Ram, *The Changing Agenda of Israeli Sociology: Theory, Ideology and Identity* (in English) (New York: State University of New York Press, 1994); and especially Ran Hacohen, "Influence of the Middle-East Peace Process on the Hebrew Language," in *Undoing and Redoing Corpus Planning*, edited by Michael Clyne (Berlin: Mouton de Gruyter, 1997).

4. Hacohen, "Influence of the Middle-East Peace Process on the Hebrew Language," 391.

5. I put the word "victory" in quotes to emphasize, yet again, that the word itself deserves both semantical and pragmatical analysis.

6. Again, this is not to deny the currently obvious adage that no descriptive word is, or can be, shorn of theory or ideology or that there are no facts divorced from values. But let us, for the moment, pretend there are.

7. See Ran Hacohen's "Influence of the Middle-East Peace Process on the Hebrew Language" for an exhaustive list of the vocabulary of occupation under the categories of "us" and "them," "armed conflict," "occupation," and references to several others.

8. A very worthwhile example of this is the renowned 1984 Kav 300 incident. When three Palestinians boarded and hijacked an Israeli bus, two of them were stopped by Israeli armed forces, captured, and taken off the bus, and later killed by the Israeli Secret Service. In Israeli jargon, these were Palestinian "terrorists" and it was a well-kept secret (for nigh on several years) that they were, apparently, unarmed. When the issue surfaced again recently (through the bravado and admission of the man who "bashed their brains in"), the *New York Times* (a purportedly neutral purveyor of words) described them as three Palestinian "unarmed youths."

9. This brings to mind CNN's routine description of southern Lebanon as "Israel's self-proclaimed security zone." Here, too, one may hear the implicit negation of this area as really being a security zone.

10. The vagaries of any philosophical (or linguistic) analysis of "current" events are such that it is by definition a function of the changing tides of history. Since the time I wrote and presented this article the political situation in the area has deteriorated so radically that certain givens of my analysis (like an ongoing peace process) have virtually disappeared. Whether the suggestions entertained in the last two sections can continue to hold water is, in part, the question of whether semantics and pragmatics are as variable as the events underlying language. At any rate, there is no telling whether at the time of publication things will have deteriorated not only as far as cessation of the peace process, but also to the point of outright war, or perhaps we will be at some more tangible process of real peace.

11. This is somewhat related to another semantical change. The term used by Zionists for this local piece of land before the emergence of the state of Israel was Palestine, which carries phonetic Hebrew connotations. This has now given way, on the Israeli Left, of course, to Palestine, which is truly Arabic.

12. In this admission, I take issue with Hacohen (see note 3), who says that "the on-going [so-called] Peace Process seems, so far, mainly to reaffirm, not change, the previous political situation" (408). On a deeper level, one may also legitimately argue the question of whether there is a real semantical change at all.

13. For systematic presentations of these concepts and their respective and comprehensive roles in linguistic theories of pragmatics, see Stephen C. Levinson, *Pragmatics* (Cambridge: Cambridge University Press, 1983); Jacob L. Mey, *Pragmatics: An Introduction* (Oxford: Blackwell, 1993).

14. See note 10.

Further Reading

Ateek, Naim Stifan. *Justice and Only Justice: A Palestinian Theology of Liberation.* Maryknoll, NY: Orbis Books, 1989.

Ateek, Naim Stifan, Marc H. Ellis, and Rosemary Radford Reuther, eds. *Faith and Intifada: Palestinian Christian Voices.* Maryknoll, NY: Orbis Books, 1992.

Boulding, Elise, ed. *Building Peace in the Middle East: Challenges for States and Civil Society.* Boulder, CO: Lynne Rienner Publishers, 1994.

Buber, Marin. *I and Thou.* Translated by Ronald Gregor Smith. New York: Scribner's, 1958.

Chomsky, Noam. *Deterring Democracy.* London: Verso, 1991.

———. *Necessary Illusions.* Boston: South End Press, 1989.

———. *Powers and Prospects.* Boston: South End Press, 1996.

———. *Turning the Tide.* Boston: South End Press, 1985.

———. *World Orders, Old and New.* New York: Columbia University Press, 1994.

Clyne, Michael, ed. *Undoing and Redoing Corpus Planning.* Berlin: Mouton de Gruyter, 1997.

Donohue, John J., and John L. Esposito, eds. *Islam in Transition: Muslim Perspectives.* Oxford: Oxford University Press, 1982.

Du Bois, W.E.B. *The Soul of Black Folk.* New York: Vantage Books, 1990.

Fanon, Frantz. *The Wretched of the Earth.* Translated by Constance Farrington. New York: Grove Press, 1963.

Gazit, Shlomo. *The Carrot and the Stick: Israel's Policy in Judea and Samaria, 1967–1968.* Washington, DC: B'nai B'rith Books, 1985.

Gordon, Haim. *Dance, Dialogue and Despair: Existentialist Philosophy and Education for Peace in Israel.* Tuscaloosa: University of Alabama Press, 1986.

―――. *Make Room for Dreams: Spiritual Challenges to Zionism*. Westport, CT: Greenwood Press, 1989.

―――. *Quicksand: Israel, the Intifada and the Rise of Political Evil in Democracies*. East Lansing: Michigan State University Press, 1995.

Gordon, Haim, and Rivca Gordon. *Israel/Palestine: The Quest for Dialogue*. Maryknoll, NY: Orbis Books, 1991.

―――. *Sartre and Evil: Guidelines for a Struggle*. Westport, CT: Greenwood Press, 1995.

Gordon, Neve, and Ruchama Marton, eds. *Torture: Human Rights, Medical Ethics and the Case of Israel*. London: Zed Books, 1995.

Harkabi, Yehoshafat. *The Palestinian Covenant and Its Meaning*. London: Vallentine, Mitchel, 1979.

Heikal, Mohamed. *The Sphinx and the Commisar: The Rise and Fall of Soviet Influence in the Middle East*. New York: Harper and Row, 1978.

Isaac, J., and H. Shuval, eds. *Water and Peace in the Middle East*. Amsterdam: Elsevier, 1994.

Kunz, Diane. *Butter and Guns: America's Cold War Economic Diplomacy*. New York: Free Press, 1997.

Langer, Felicia. *An Age of Stone*. Translated by Isaac Cohen. London: Quartet Books, 1988.

Levinson, Stephen C. *Pragmatics*. Cambridge: Cambridge University Press, 1983.

Lukacs, Yehuda, ed. *Documents on the Israeli-Palestinian Conflict, 1967–1983*. Cambridge: Cambridge University Press, 1984.

Lyotard, Jean-François. *The Post-Modern Condition: A Report on Knowledge*. Translated by G. Bennington and B. Massumi. Minneapolis: University of Minnesota Press, 1984.

Madison, G. B. *The Hermeneutics of Postmodernism*. Indianapolis: Indiana University Press, 1988.

Mendes-Flohr, Paul R. *A Land of Two People: Martin Buber on Jews and Arabs*. Oxford: Oxford University Press, 1983.

Morris, Benny. *The Birth of the Palestinian Refugee Problem, 1947–1949*. Cambridge: Cambridge University Press, 1987.

―――. *1948 and After: Israel and the Palestinians*. Oxford: Oxford University Press, 1994.

Painter, David. *Oil and the American Century*. Baltimore: Johns Hopkins University Press, 1986.

Rabe, Stephen. *The Road to OPEC*. Austin: University of Texas Press, 1982.

Ram, Uri. *The Changing Agenda of Israeli Sociology: Theory, Ideology and Identity*. Albany, NY: State University of New York Press, 1994.

Rosencrance, Richard, and Arthur A. Stein, eds. *The Domestic Basis of Grand Strategy*. Ithaca, NY: Cornell University Press, 1993.

Roy, Sara. *The Gaza Strip: The Political Economy of De-development*. Washington, DC: Institute for Palestine Studies, 1995.

Safran, Nadav. *Israel: The Embattled Ally.* Cambridge, MA: Harvard University Press, 1978.

Said, Edward W. *Peace and Its Discontents.* New York: Vintage Books, 1996.

Schwedler, Jillian, ed. *Toward Civil Society in the Middle East.* Boulder, CO: Lynne Rienner Publishers, 1995.

Williamson, Murray, MacGregor Know, and Alvin Bernstein, eds. *The Making of Strategy: Rulers, States and War.* Cambridge: Cambridge University Press, 1994.

Wittgenstein, Ludwig. *The Blue and Brown Books.* Oxford: Basil Blackwell, 1958.

———. *Philosophical Investigations.* Translated by G.E.M. Anscombe. Oxford: Basil Blackwell, 1963.

Index

Contributors

ARYEH ARNON, Economics, Ben-Gurion University of the Negev, Beer Sheva.

ANAT BILETZKI, Philosophy, Tel Aviv University, Tel Aviv.

MUSA BUDAIRI, Humanities, El Kuds University, Jerusalem.

NOAM CHOMSKY, Linguistics, MIT, Cambridge, MA.

YEHEZKEL DROR, Political Science, Hebrew University, Jerusalem.

HAIM GORDON, Education, Ben-Gurion University of the Negev, Beer Sheva.

TAMAR GOZANSKY, The Knesset, Jerusalem.

RUCHAMA MARTON, Physicians for Human Rights and Tel Aviv University, Tel Aviv.

ANAT MATAR, Philosophy, Tel Aviv University, Tel Aviv.

PAUL MENDES-FLOHR, Jewish Thought, Hebrew University, Jerusalem.

ILAN PAPPE, History, Haifa University, Haifa.

NADERA SHALHOUB-KEVORKIAN, Law, Hebrew University, Jerusalem.

LEON SHELEFF, Law, Tel Aviv University, Tel Aviv.

MOSHE ZUCKERMANN, History, Tel Aviv University, Tel Aviv.